How to Buy a House
The Right Way

The Complete Home Buying Guide
For First-Time Home Buyers and
Seasoned Pros

Part of the *Smart Living* Series by:

Mark Kennedy

Liability Disclaimer

How to Buy a House
The Right Way

The Complete Home Buying Guide For First-Time Home Buyers and Seasoned Pros

If you think you can do it, or you think you can't do it, you are right.

-Henry Ford

Table of Contents

Introduction

Many renters would like to buy a home of their own. Some are not sure how to do it, and others think that homeownership is out of their reach. Many current homeowners would like to buy a new home, but dread going through the home buying process again. The good news is that home buying does not have to be a difficult or unpleasant experience.

My name is Mark Kennedy. I first entered the mortgage industry in 1991 and I've helped both first-timers and seasoned pros buy or build their dream homes. I've heard more horror stories about the home buying process than I care to remember. And, I have realized one thing: most of the time those horror stories could have been prevented by the buyer being better educated about the process.

It does not matter if you have never bought a home, or if you have bought several. In fact, I often see those who have bought several homes in the past make the biggest mistakes. Typically, this is because they think they know it all and they ignore the good lessons they have learned from their past experiences. So, whether you are a first-timer or repeat offender, you must be an educated buyer.

If you take action and follow the best practices outlined in this book, your home buying experience will be considerably enhanced. You will be armed with all the tools you need to find and buy the home of your dreams.

The seasoned pros reading this book will be best served by taking the lessons from their previous buying experiences and combining them with the ideas and best practices discussed here. It will make your next purchase go considerably smoother.

First-timers, you must first make the decision that you really do want to own a home of your own. Even if you think your finances or credit are not quite ready for such a large transaction, you need to set the goal of home-ownership for yourself. You have actually already taken the first step just reading this book.

Look around you - at your friends, neighbors and coworkers. Many of them represent someone just like you who claim they want a home of their own but wouldn't take the initiative, wouldn't invest the time, or were just too lazy or scared to read this book.

But you did. And, as a reward, you will soon reach your goals of homeownership if you wish.

You managed to put aside all the things that could have distracted you: work, the kids, watching football or the latest fad TV show. Whatever; you managed to put all of that aside to start today. I'm proud of you and you should be proud of yourselves.

Now, I have a few important questions…

- Why are you reading this today?
- What attracted you to purchase this book?
- What motivated you to set aside all other activities to start reading it right now?

For some of you it was just curiosity. Just a small itch, a mild thought like, "I've heard we are in the best "buyer's" market in history, so I may as well take a look."

Or, maybe "it would be good to get out of that apartment," "stop paying rent," "own a home of my own" or "upgrade to my dream home."

For others of you it is a need. A need for more space, privacy or security, a need for a tax break, a need to be independent, to have the freedom that only a home of your own can give you.

And, for some of you it is a Dream.

It's a dream that keeps you up at night. A dream, or even a burning desire, to tell your landlord exactly what they can do with their lousy maintenance service and ever increasing rent.

An exquisitely exciting thought of telling your too-loud neighbors to scream all they want to - you're out of here.

It's a desire to get your full share of

The American Dream

Well, whether you are reading this just out of curiosity or because you have a deep down burning desire to make a better life for yourself and your family - you're at the right place.

My job is to help give you the knowledge and information you need to overcome whatever obstacles have kept you from owning the home of your dreams.

After nearly 20 years as a mortgage professional working with individuals like you and families like yours, I have discovered the primary reason most people do not own a home of their own or take advantage of moving up to a newer or different home:

That reason is:

Life Happens.

This may sound simplistic, and it is in many ways. What I really mean is, that despite your best intentions to buy a home, any number of things just seem to get in the way. Maybe you have not been able to save for a down payment. The good news is, as I will explain later, that you don't need a huge down payment to buy a home – even in 2012.

Or, maybe you have the down payment, but think you cannot qualify for the mortgage loan. After all, there are plenty of good, honest, hardworking people out there who, through youthful ignorance, lack of planning, or just plain bad luck, have credit issues that keep them from being able to qualify for a home. If you fall into this category, fear not. With a little effort you can correct any issues you may have and get yourself back on track in just a few months. I'll explain more in Chapter 3.

On top of that, our royally screwed up credit system in this country has actually made it more difficult than ever to buy a home in 2012, despite being in the biggest "buyer's" market in our history and despite the record low interest rates that are available. Now, more than ever, you need to fully understand the home buying process and the mortgage process in order to take advantage of today's market. This book can help you arm yourself with the knowledge you need to successfully navigate the home buying process, while avoiding the pitfalls and traps that abound.

After a brief discussion of the benefits of home ownership, we will explain the mortgage process in detail. Then, we will discuss several insider tips, secrets and traps to avoid in the home buying process.

So, with this in mind - let's get started.

Chapter 1
Reaching for the American Dream
2012 and Beyond – Why Should You Buy a Home Now

Whether you are a first time buyer or not; now is the time to buy a home! The better you understand the reasons behind that statement, the less daunting the entire process will appear to you. Here are several good reasons why you should buy a home.

1. Buyer's market

We are in the midst of the biggest and best buyer's market in the last 70 years. Simply put, there is no better time to buy a new home. With historically high foreclosure rates and the drastic "burst of the housing bubble," those who are able to buy now will get the best deals in their lifetime. Most experts agree that the market has yet to bottom, but may be close, so the window of opportunity is now.

2. Pride of Ownership

Pride of ownership is the number one reason why people yearn to own their home. It means you can paint the walls any color you desire, turn up the volume on your CD player, attach permanent fixtures and decorate your home according to your own taste. Home ownership gives you and your family a sense of stability and security. It's making an investment in your future.

15

3. Appreciation

Although the real estate market has been hard hit in the last couple years, real estate moves in cycles, sometimes up, sometimes down. But, over the years, real estate has consistently appreciated. Buying now – at the bottom of the market – virtually guarantees that your home will appreciate over the next decade and beyond.

4. Mortgage Interest Deductions

Home ownership is a superb tax shelter and our tax rates favor homeowners. As long as your mortgage balance is smaller than the price of your home, mortgage interest is fully deductible on your tax return. Interest is the largest component of your mortgage payment. Those who have never owned a home may not realize the incredible tax advantages they are missing out on. The mortgage tax deduction can be a huge tax savings for you, meaning a nice (or nicer) refund each year.

5. Tax Deductions & Preferential Tax Treatment

Real estate property taxes paid on your first home are fully deductible for income tax purposes. Additionally, many of the costs associated with buying the home are deductible. The IRS loves homeowners! And, if you receive more profit than the allowable exclusion upon sale of your home, that profit will be considered a capital asset as long as you owned your home for more than one year. Capital assets receive preferential tax treatment.

6. Capital Gain Exclusion

As long as you have lived in your home for two of the past five years, you can exclude up to $250,000 for an individual or $500,000 for a married couple of profit from capital gains. You do not have to buy a replacement home or move up. There is no age restriction, and the "over-55" rule does not apply. You can exclude the above thresholds from taxes every 24 months, which means you could sell every two years and pocket your profit--subject to limitation--free from taxation.

7. Home Owners Are Wealthier Than Renters

Simply put, those who own their own homes build more wealth than those who rent. See what the Federal Reserve Board says in Chapter 2.

8. Mortgage Reduction Builds Equity

Each month, part of your monthly payment is applied to the principal balance of your loan, which reduces your obligation. The way amortization works, the principal portion of your principal and interest payment increases slightly every month. It is lowest on your first payment and highest on your last payment. Over time, you will build significant equity (and wealth) just by making your housing payment.

Chapter 2
The Benefits of Home Ownership

What is it about home ownership that is so appealing?

First and foremost it is the true AMERICAN DREAM – but why?

Think about that for a moment – what is it about home ownership that stirs so many people's blood?

A moment ago, I asked you to visualize what you want for your family. The chances are very good that, of the many things that may have crossed your mind, much of those goals could be solved by home ownership.

Owning a home can provide you with:

- Privacy
- Space
- Financial Freedom
- Security
- Better environment for your kids
- Tax Break

There are as many great reasons people want a home of their own as there are houses on the market.

In our home, when I was growing up, Saturday night was always cookout night. My dad would fire up the grill and cook steaks, burgers, ribs, or dogs (whatever mood we were in). The whole family spent the evening eating, talking, laughing and having a great time.

After I grew up and moved away, I really missed those Saturday night cookouts. I couldn't wait until I had a house of my own with a backyard and a grill so I could start that tradition with my family.

Today, thanks to owning our own home, Saturday nights at our house are just like they were for me 30-some years ago (but don't tell my dad – I'm a better cook!!). My kids now look forward to our cookouts as much as I once did.

So, let me ask you a couple of questions...

- Do you love the smell of a big, fat, juicy steak or burger sizzling on the grill?
- Do you love to barbeque?
- Do you savor moments with your friends and family?

We had a long holiday weekend just a few weeks ago.

Were you at home, in your apartment, that weekend?

Were YOU able to participate in that true All-American pastime of grilling or barbecuing your favorite foods in your own backyard that weekend?

You know most apartment complexes, and many other landlords, won't even let you grill out on a holiday weekend much less a Saturday night.

THAT'S UN-AMERICAN !!!!!

It's also un-American to pay too much in income taxes – you get no tax breaks when you rent, but you do in a home of your own.

It's un-American to continue to throw away money month after month just to have a place to live.

It's un-American to have to lug groceries half a block, then up a flight of stairs in the rain.

That's not the American Dream!

In most rentals you can't paint the walls another color. What would the landlord say?

You can't even bang a nail in the wall to hang a picture without some landlord's or management company's permission.

That's not living. That's not freedom – and America was built on freedom.

More Benefits of Home Ownership

Home owners provide stability. Owners typically stay in their home 12 years whereas renters stay no more than three years, according to the U.S. Census's American Housing Survey.

Home ownership builds confidence. Owners possess significantly higher levels of self-confidence than renters. (Rossi and Weber National Survey of Families).

Home owners create positive environments for families. Children of home owners are 59% more likely to become homeowners. Their children are also 25% more likely to graduate from high school and 116% more likely to graduate from college. (Boehm & Schlottmann, University of Tennessee).

Home ownership builds wealth. Check out the chart below provided by the Federal Reserve Board. Simply put, home-ownership builds wealth!

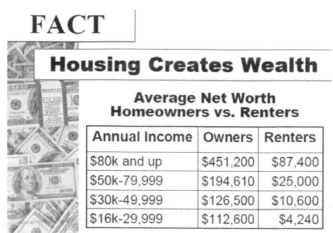

FACT

Housing Creates Wealth

Average Net Worth
Homeowners vs. Renters

Annual Income	Owners	Renters
$80k and up	$451,200	$87,400
$50k-79,999	$194,610	$25,000
$30k-49,999	$126,500	$10,600
$16k-29,999	$112,600	$4,240

Source – Federal Reserve Board

Home ownership also provides tax benefits. The typical home owner that pays a $1,000 house payment will realize tax savings of about $120 each month.

Home ownership improves neighborhoods. Owners are 28% more likely to improve their home and 10% more likely to participate in solving local problems. (George Galster, "Land Economics" and DiPasquale & Glaeser, Harvard's Joint Center for Housing Studies).

Home owners are more involved in civic affairs: including voting in the last election and knowing their elected officials. (DiPasquale & Glaeser, Harvard's Joint Center for Housing Studies).

Are You Being Ripped Off By Paying Rent?

Think about what you pay in rent each month.

Are you paying $900 a month? Over $1,000 a month?

Have you been renting for two or three (or more) years?

If you have, the chances are that you have paid your landlord well over $24,000 dollars and have nothing to show for it. And, if you are paying over $1,000 a month, those numbers sky rocket.

How many years have you been renting? Fill that in on the line below and multiply by 12 and write the answer in the space provided.

_____ (years) X 12 (months) = _____

Now multiply your rent amount by the number of months you've been renting.

_____ (monthly rent) X _____ (# of months) = _____

The number you calculate is the amount of money you've given to your landlord and literally wasted.

And what do you have to show for it?

- No Equity
- No Tax Break
- No Privacy
- Not even a grilled hot dog

Now, take a look at the chart below. Think about how much you could have saved, or how much wealth and equity you could have by now.

How Much Money Have You Lost By Paying Rent?

Monthly Rent	Year 1	Year 2	Year 3	Year 4	Year 5
$500	$ 6,000	$ 12,000	$ 18,000	$ 24,000	$ 30,000
$550	$ 6,600	$ 13,200	$ 19,800	$ 26,400	$ 33,000
$600	$ 7,200	$ 14,400	$ 21,600	$ 28,800	$ 36,000
$650	$ 7,800	$ 15,600	$ 23,400	$ 31,200	$ 39,000
$700	$ 8,400	$ 16,800	$ 25,200	$ 33,600	$ 42,000
$750	$ 9,000	$ 18,000	$ 27,000	$ 36,000	$ 45,000
$800	$ 9,600	$ 19,200	$ 28,800	$ 38,400	$ 48,000
$850	$ 10,200	$ 20,400	$ 30,600	$ 40,800	$ 51,000
$900	$ 10,800	$ 21,600	$ 32,400	$ 43,200	$ 54,000
$950	$ 11,400	$ 22,800	$ 34,200	$ 45,600	$ 57,000
$1000	$ 12,000	$ 24,000	$ 36,000	$ 48,000	$ 60,000
$1050	$ 12,600	$ 25,200	$ 37,800	$ 50,400	$ 63,000
$1100	$ 13,200	$ 26,400	$ 39,600	$ 52,800	$ 66,000
$1150	$ 13,800	$ 27,600	$ 41,400	$ 55,200	$ 69,000
$1200	$ 14,400	$ 28,800	$ 43,200	$ 57,600	$ 72,000
$1250	$ 15,000	$ 30,000	$ 45,000	$ 60,000	$ 75,000
$1300	$ 15,600	$ 31,200	$ 46,800	$ 62,400	$ 78,000
$1350	$ 16,200	$ 32,400	$ 48,600	$ 64,800	$ 81,000
$1400	$ 16,800	$ 33,600	$ 50,400	$ 67,200	$ 84,000
$1450	$ 17,400	$ 34,800	$ 52,200	$ 69,600	$ 87,000
$1500	$ 18,000	$ 36,000	$ 54,000	$ 72,000	$ 90,000
$1600	$ 19,200	$ 38,400	$ 57,600	$ 76,800	$ 93,000
$1700	$ 20,400	$ 40,800	$ 61,200	$ 81,600	$ 96,000
$1800	$ 21,600	$ 43,200	$ 64,800	$ 86,400	$ 99,200
$1900	$ 22,800	$ 46,600	$ 68,400	$ 91,200	$102,000
$2000	$ 24,000	$ 48,000	$ 72,000	$ 96,000	$105,000

In the Monthly Rent Column find how much you are paying in rent.

Then move Right to the Column for the number of years you have been renting.

That is how much money you have paid your landlord that could have been going toward a home of your own.

By breaking out of rental prison, you will be able to build wealth for yourself, as well as enjoy all of the other benefits that go with home ownership.

How Much Home Can You Afford?

Buying a home involves understanding your available down payment as well as your potential monthly payments (remember, your monthly payment equals your loan principal payment + interest + monthly property taxes + monthly property insurance + any mortgage insurance (if you put less than 20% down). This is your "PITI").

When you start thinking about buying a home, a natural first question is: "how much home can I afford?"

And the answer is: "It depends." It depends on:

- Your verifiable income.
- Your monthly debts.
- Your credit scores.
- The loan programs chosen.

Your income and monthly debts are the major factors, as this will determine how much monthly payment you can handle (and therefore the amount of loan and purchase price). Remember, your income must be verifiable. The days of "stated income" and "no income" loans are gone for the most part. Although, it is certain that they will be back again at some point in the future, once Wall Street greed causes the banks to forget the mess that was created the last time these loans were allowed. It's just a matter of time. But for now (2012), income must be fully verified for most loan programs.

Also, another note on income: if you are self-employed, earn commissions, or have a part time job, you must have a full 24 month history of that income in order for it to count towards qualifying.

Your monthly debts include any payments you currently have for financed items (cars, credit cards, installment loans, etc.) and any payments being deducted from your pay stubs, such as child support or alimony. They do not include your utility or phone bills, car insurance, or other regular living expenses, unless they show up on your credit report. Typically, any installment loan (not credit cards) that has less than 10 months of payments remaining will not be counted. However, you need to check with the specific loan's guidelines about this policy, as this has been one of the many areas of change over the last couple years and many programs now include all installment debt regardless of remaining balance.

Your credit scores are also considered to some extent, as some loan programs will allow you to stretch your qualifying amounts if you have excellent credit and some programs will reduce those amounts if you have less than perfect credit.

And, finally, every loan program out there has slightly different guidelines. These guidelines determine, among other things, the amount of acceptable debt to monthly income the loan type will allow.

Mortgage lenders calculate "ratios" to determine the amount of payment for which you will qualify. The "ratio" is simply your ratio of debts to income. In the case of buying a home; it would be your projected new debts to your income. This allows lenders to determine whether they think you can make the payment or not. Remember, all loan programs are slightly different so the example below is just a rough guideline.

Typically, there is a "front ratio" and a "back ratio" involved in the process, although some loans simply use the back ratio as the only ratio they evaluate. The front ratio is the projected house payment (PITI) divided by your monthly income. The back ratio is your projected house payment (PITI) *plus* your monthly debts divided by your monthly income. In order to qualify for the loan, you must fit under both these ratios.

Let's say your income is $7,000 per month total and your monthly debts are $1,250 per month. A typical loan program may allow ratios of 29/41 (remember, some are stricter, such as 28/36, etc.), meaning that your maximum front ratio can be 29% of your monthly income and your maximum back ratio can be 41% of your monthly income. So, in this example, $7,000 * .29 = $2,030; and $7,000 * .41 = $2,870. Now, according to the front ratio, you could have a total monthly house payment (PITI) of up to $2,030 per month.

But, your monthly debts are $1250 and your back ratio limits your total of house + debt to be $2,870. So, the lender would look at your back ratio, in this case, as the determining factor of your maximum allowable payment: $2,870 - $1,250 = $1,620 maximum house payment (PITI).

To determine the maximum loan for which you can qualify and the maximum house price you can buy, you would now need to know a close estimate of:

- The loan interest rate.

- The projected monthly taxes (get this from your county tax board).
- The monthly property insurance cost (get this from your insurance agent).
- Any monthly mortgage insurance (PMI), if putting less than 20% down (get this from your mortgage professional). PMI can run anywhere from about .6% to 1%+ of your loan amount per year, depending on loan program and guidelines. Divide this by 12 to get the monthly amount.
- The amount of your down payment.

So, for example, if you find out that monthly property taxes for a particular house are $200 (remember, this is based on the home's assessed value and the tax rate itself will vary *massively* from county to county and state to state) and the property insurance cost is $75 a month and you are putting $20,000 down (less than 20%, so you will also need PMI); you can back into a maximum loan amount and house price. Remember, you will not be able to get an exact figure until you know the correct amounts for PMI and the other figures, so it is wise to overestimate these costs when doing this estimate.

If, as in our example, you are allowed $1,620 in PITI, this means that the amount you would be allowed for your actual loan would be: $1,620 - $200 - $75 - $200 (high estimate for PMI) = $1,145 maximum principal and interest (the actual loan payment). And, if interest rates are 5.5%, you can now use a mortgage calculator to find that the maximum loan balance for which you qualify would be approximately $201,600. Obviously, as interest rates go lower you will be able to qualify for more home and as they go higher, you will qualify for a smaller loan and therefore a less expensive home.

Based on the buyer putting $20,000 down, we would now know that they can shop for homes that cost approximately $220,000 (maximum qualified loan amount + down payment).

Now, let's compare the above example to the same person with $7,000 income, but who has zero debt. Using the above numbers, the back ratio would not be the determining factor since there is no additional monthly debt. So, the lender would use the front ratio calculation in this case (or in the case of loan programs that only use one ratio, just that one ratio). Now, our buyer would be able to qualify for a more expensive home: $2,030 maximum PITI - $200-$75-$200 = $1,555 maximum loan payment. At 5.5% interest, this would mean they can finance up to approximately $273,000. Add the $20,000 down payment and they can now shop for homes in the $293,000 range.

As you can see, it is crucial to avoid large debts if you want to qualify for the most home. This same person in our example is forced into a $70,000 less home due to their monthly debts.

PLEASE READ THIS WARNING:

A word of advice from a 20-year financial veteran: other than poor credit, huge car payments are the number one thing that hurts mortgage qualifications.

It is much, much easier to qualify for car loans than mortgages. And, for some misguided reason, people seem to think they should have (and can qualify for) these massive car payments being sold by car dealers. This is fine if you plan to live in your car, but for most of us this is not the long-term plan.

Here is a rule of thumb for car payments (you will probably not like this, but the truth hurts sometimes): do not allow yourself to have total car payments equal to more than 7% MAXIMUM of your actual, verifiable income. This would mean our example buyer with the $7,000 total income can handle up to about $490 in car payments MAXIMUM if they want to maintain a healthy financial outlook. That is the MAXIMUM you should allow yourself.

It is important to go through a quick exercise like this to determine how much house you can shop for, so you do not waste your time with, or get excited about, homes you cannot afford.

Now, here is one last "quick and dirty" rule of thumb that you can use instead of going through the more precise calculations above. For most people with moderate debt (about 10% of their monthly income); you can likely afford a home that costs up to about three times your verified annual household income. If you have little to no debt and can put 20% down you can probably buy a house worth closer to four times your verified annual household income.

As a comparison to the results we go above, our example buyer that earns $84,000 a year would qualify for home price of about $252,000 using this quick and dirty method, which is a bit more than the $220,000 we got above. But, our example buyer had more than about 10% in debt (closer to 18%) so you can see that you have to be careful using this method. If you have a reasonable debt load, this method can at least give you an idea where to start shopping.

Finally, we have left out one important thing -- closing costs. You'll need to make sure that you account for paying the closing costs on the loan. This is *in addition to* the amount you put down as the down payment. When deciding how much you have available for a down payment, be sure to account for the fact that you will have to pay closing costs.

Often, especially in a buyer's market like we are currently experiencing (2012), you can negotiate for the seller to pay some, or most, of your closing costs. Most loan programs allow the seller to pay up to 3% of the sale price towards the buyer's closing costs, and some allow up to 6%. Very few loan programs today allow you to borrow more than the cost of the house so that you can roll in the closing costs into your loan amount.

Your "closing costs" are typically made up of a couple things: your actual costs to obtain the loan (these are technically what "closing costs" are), plus your required "pre-paid" items. Pre-paid items include any amounts that you will need to pay in advance to establish your loan escrow amounts for property taxes and insurance. These are determined by each loan program, but you should expect that you will have to make these deposits at closing (which is why most people call them closing costs, although they are really deposits into your own account to pay for future expenses). These closing costs and pre-paid items can really add up, so you must be prepared for them.

These can include some or all of the following:

- Appraisal (can be up to $600+). This is paid to the appraisal company to confirm the fair market value of the home. Typically you will pay this in advance, not at closing, but it is considered a closing cost and you will see it listed as a credit for being paid in advance on your closing documents.
- Credit Report (can be up to $30). A Tri-merge credit report is pulled to get your credit history and score. You cannot supply your own credit report.
- Closing Fee or Escrow Fee (generally calculated at about $2.00 per thousand of purchase price plus $250, although this varies greatly). This is paid to the Title Company, Escrow Company or attorney for conducting the closing. The Title Company or escrow oversees the closing as an independent party in your home purchase.

Some states require a real estate attorney be present at every closing, which adds to your cost.

- Title Company, Title Search or Exam Fee (varies greatly, usually about $100) - This fee is paid to the title company for doing a thorough search of the property's records. The title company researches the deed to your new home, ensuring that no one else has a claim to the property.
- Survey Fee (up to $400). This fee goes to a survey company to verify all property lines and things like shared fences on the property. This is not required in all states or by all loan programs.
- Flood Determination or Life of Loan Coverage (up to $20). This is paid to a third party to determine if the property is located in a flood zone. If the property is found to be located within a flood zone, you will need to buy flood insurance. The insurance, of course, is paid separately.
- Courier Fees (up to $50) - This covers the cost of transporting documents to complete the loan transaction as quickly as possible.
- Lender's Policy Title Insurance (Calculated from the purchase price and varies by Title Company). This is insurance to assure the lender that you own the home and the lender's mortgage is a valid lien. Similar to the title search, but sometimes a separate line item.
- Owner's Policy Title Insurance (Calculated from the purchase price and varies by Title Company). This is an insurance policy protecting you in the event someone challenges your ownership of the home.
- Natural Hazards Disclosure Report. Required by law in the state of California for the seller to give the buyer.

Reports cost from $90 to $150. May be required by other states

- Homeowners' Insurance ($300 and up, depending on your state, the insurance company you choose and the value of the home). This covers possible damages to your home. Your first year's insurance is often paid at closing as a "pre-paid."
- Buyer's Attorney Fee (not required in all states - $400 and up).
- Lender's Attorney Fee (not required in all states - $150 and up).
- Escrow Deposit for Property Taxes & Mortgage Insurance (varies widely). Often you are asked to put down several months of property tax and mortgage insurance payments at closing (another "pre-paid").
- Transfer Taxes (varies widely by state & municipality). This is the tax paid when the title passes from seller to buyer.
- Recording Fees (varies widely depending on municipality) - A fee charged by your local recording office, usually city or county, for the recording of public land records.
- Processing Fee (up to $1,000). This goes to your lender. It reimburses the cost to process the information on your loan application.
- Underwriting Fee (up to $1,000). This also goes to your lender, covering the cost of researching whether or not to approve you for the loan.
- Loan Discount Points (often zero to two percent+ of loan amount). "Points" are the fee paid to the lender as their fee to do the loan for you. One point is one percent of your loan amount. Typically, the more "points" you pay, the lower interest rate you will get.

- Pre-Paid Interest (varies depending on loan amount, interest rate and time of month you close on your loan). This is money you pay at closing in order to get the interest paid up through the first of the month. Also part of the "pre-paid" items.
- Property Tax (usually up to 6 months of county property tax). Another "pre-paid" item.
- Wood Destroying Pest Inspection and Allocation of Costs (Termite Report). If required by the lender or buyer, the inspection generally runs up to $125.00. Repairs can get expensive if evidence of termites, dry rot or other wood damage is found. Typically, any repairs are paid by the seller before closing.
- Home Owners Association Transfer Fees. The Seller will pay for this transfer which will show that the dues are paid current, what the dues are, a copy of the association financial statements, minutes and notices. The buyer should review these documents to determine if the Association has enough reserves in place to avoid future special assessments, check to see if there are special assessments, legal action, or any other items that might be of concern. Also included will be Association by-laws, rules and regulations and CC & Rs. The fee for the transfer varies per association, but generally around $200-$300.

As you can see, the list of potential closing costs and pre-paid items is extensive and can really add up. You must be prepared for these costs or you will find yourself unable to close on the loan. As mentioned, these costs vary greatly from loan program to loan program; from state to state; and from lender to lender. It is impossible to give you an exact amount to expect to pay, but a rough estimate may be to expect to pay up to 5% of the purchase price for these items at the high end. And more if you are paying additional discount points to lower your interest rate. Negotiating to have the seller pay for some or all of these costs is a good idea if you can do so.

Chapter 3
Problem Credit Does Not Have
to be a Problem For Long

Credit problems affect tens of millions of people in America today. If you find yourself among them, please know that you are in good company and that there is a light at the end of the tunnel. Solutions are available, and they are not always quick and easy. But they are very, very possible. In fact, with the right plan, most people, no matter their current situation, can have the credit restored and mortgage eligible within six to twelve months.

Education, patience and perseverance are all needed to successfully navigate your journey towards higher credit scores and financial independence.

Not many people choose to have bad credit; it is usually the result of factors beyond their control. Loss of income, medical emergency, or family upheavals can happen all too often to decent, hard-working people who would never even consider paying a bill late during normal circumstances. Sure, there are certainly plenty of lazy, irresponsible people out there who simply ignore their obligations.

More likely, an event beyond your control caused a situation where it became difficult, or even impossible, to cover all of your financial obligations. And the result was credit scores that are less than ideal.

No matter the reason for a person's credit issues, there are three basic, yet crucial, steps that must be taken on the path to better credit.

I.   *Education:* It is important to understand what happened and how to fix it. Your education must begin with a careful analysis of your situation and the events that lead you here, and continue with knowing how to fix the problems and prevent them from ever happening again. Credit education never ends.

II.   *Patience:* You must develop a sound and comprehensive plan to begin fixing the problems. This includes understanding that all credit fixes are not quick and easy. Depending on your specific circumstances, you may need to allow several months, or even a year or more, to reach your credit goals.

III.   *Perseverance:* In every case, you must stick with your credit repair program until you reach your goals. Then, when you do, you must be diligent about maintaining your credit rating.

Remember, credit repair is not quick and easy – and it is crucial to stick with it and even seek professional help if needed. The good news is that most people can significantly and drastically affect their credit ratings with a little time, effort and know-how. In fact, many people can achieve 100 point plus increases to their scores in only six months.

It is important to understand that even short term financial difficulties can have a long-term impact on your credit profile and credit scores. Paying bills late, skipping payments or overusing credit cards will all get reported to the credit bureaus as negative items. This, then, ends up on your credit report and can remain there for a very long time.

The information on your credit report is then used by the bureaus to generate a credit score – typically referred to as a "FICO" score. Current and potential future lenders then use these scores to decide your credit worthiness.

Those with the highest scores will be offered the best rates and terms on credit cards and other loans. These are considered A+

or "prime" candidates. Those with average or below average credit profiles will pay much higher fees and rates in order to get the same access to credit as the prime customers.

And, those who ruin their credit profiles and have low credit scores find that they cannot qualify for credit at any reasonable terms, if at all. Access to things like credit cards, car loans, mortgages, home equity loans and even department store credit will all be severely limited. In the twenty-first century, this is a difficult way to live.

We live in a society that relies on the use of credit. As such, it is imperative to learn how to properly manage the credit you have and protect your credit rating. It is also important to understand how to correct past credit issues, build new positive credit, and not repeat previous mistakes. Remember, the negative information listed in your credit report can remain there for seven (for regular credit issues) to fifteen years (for items like tax liens). This can severely impact your future financial stability for many years. But, there is good news: with a little education, time, and effort you can restore your credit health and live a more stress-free and financially independent life.

Credit repair and restoration is not easy. But it is very possible. It is also something than requires patience and perseverance if you wish to be successful. You also must be realistic in your goals. Do not expect to increase your scores 200 points in the next 30 or 60 days. Remember: *education, patience, and perseverance.*

This book does not have the space to go into a complete credit repair and restoration course. But, if you find yourself in a situation where you need either major or minor credit repair, I have you covered. In my *Credit Repair Black Book* (Back to School Press, 2011, available on the Amazon website in both paperback and Kindle versions), I reveal the secrets of the credit bureaus learned in my twenty years as a financial industry insider.

In The Credit Repair Black Book, you will learn to understand how the credit system works and will reveal many of the insider secrets that credit bureaus don't want you to know. In addition, it will help guide you towards managing your credit profile for maximum scores and show you how to legally and ethically restore your credit report.

The book starts with an overview of the credit reporting and scoring system. Then, we will move on to the specific secrets and tactics needed to restore and maintain a healthy credit report. Finally, as a summary, we will share over 100 insider credit tips to help maximize your scores and have a more stress-free financial outlook. This is the information formerly reserved only for financial insiders.

Credit Resource:

The Credit Repair

Black Book

Credit Repair Secrets and Strategies
the Credit Bureaus Won't Tell You
3rd *Edition, 2011*

By Mark A. Kennedy

Available on Amazon in Paperback or Kindle

Chapter 4
The Sad Truth about Most
Mortgage Brokers
(and How You Know Who You Can Trust)

Unfortunately, the mortgage lending industry is filled with less-than-reputable individuals. It seems that no matter where you turn, you find dishonest or incompetent people asking you to trust them with what may be the largest financial transaction you will ever make. Please understand I am not saying every mortgage broker or lender is dishonest or dumb; in fact, I know plenty of smart, honest and very capable mortgage professionals. It is just that there are far too many bad apples in our orchard.

Let's face it, much of the real estate and financial crash of the last couple of years was caused – at least in part – by greedy and dishonest mortgage lenders who cared only about lining their own pockets instead of actually helping their clients.

Of course, there is plenty of blame to go around, but as someone who has been on the front lines of mortgage lending since 1991, I have seen far too many people get "sold" by their mortgage lender on loans that they could not afford and/or would end up costing them a small fortune when it came time to pay off the mortgage.

How many of you know someone who had a mortgage lender try to sell them a "1%" (or close to that) loan (called an "option arm" or a "negative amortization arm") or an ARM with easy qualifying (a subprime loan)? I'll bet many of you did.

So, the question is "how do you find a loan officer you can trust?" If it were me who was looking for a loan – knowing what I know after nearly 20 years in this business – I would do the following:

1) When you speak with a mortgage professional, first and foremost, make sure you are comfortable with them. If you feel rushed or pressured in any way, move on. You should seek to work with someone who takes the time to get know and understand your needs, problems, and goals. If you ever feel like you are being "sold to" or if you sense any "red flags," it is best to find another professional.

2) If you are being quoted a rate before you have a chance to discuss your entire situation with your lender, you should be prepared for the mortgage lender's "bait and switch." There is no way possible to give someone an honest and accurate rate quote without knowing the borrower's full, complete profile. That means fully underwriting a complete application.

What will likely happen, when you are disappointed with the actual rate you are offered, is that you will hear something along the lines of "well, your situation changed…" or "as it turns out, you don't qualify for that rate…" There are two reasons to avoid this situation. The first is that when someone immediately quotes a rate, they may be setting you up for a bait and switch. If they are doing this, it is easy to understand why you should avoid them. Now, remember, all mortgage lenders have "rate sheets" (computerized these days, but they used to be actual sheets of paper with all of the available rates listed) and are able to quote a rate right away. What you need to know is that there is a better than good chance that you will not get that rate. Being fully prepared is your best weapon.

The second reason is a little less obvious: if a lender quotes you a rate without learning about your qualifications and needs, they may very well be honest – just dumb. If they are being honest and trying to give you rates before they have your info, it just may be because they don't know what they are doing. And, why would you want to work with someone who doesn't know their job?

In either case, if you are hearing rates before you are hearing questions, avoid that lender.

Now, to be fair to your mortgage professional, don't be one of those shoppers who just calls around asking "what's your rate?" as soon as someone answers the phone. Quite honestly, those borrowers who do this deserve to be taken advantage of. When someone called my office with this immediate question, I typically tried to educate them on why this is not the proper way to shop for a mortgage. If they resisted the advice, they were simply referred on to another lender. So, please remember, don't invite these kind of problems by being an uneducated shopper.

3) Make sure you are given the chance to ask any and all questions and be sure you are satisfied with the answers. If you sense that the person you are speaking to is withholding information for any reason, it is probably a good idea to move on.

4) Finally, seek to work with someone who is experienced, has direct access to a wide variety of loan programs, and has direct access to underwriting decisions. There is no reason to pay for a middleman, who will only mark-up your costs and add a layer of delay to the process. This means working with an actual lender as opposed to a broker. It also helps to work with someone who has a positive working relationship with your

Realtor. But, at the same time, do not simply take the Realtor's referral without doing your own, complete homework. This is too big a transaction to be lazy.

How Do You Get The Best Rates?

First, make sure you are comparing current mortgage rates for the same type of mortgage. Mortgage rates and closing costs can change significantly from one day to another (even hour to hour when the financial markets are moving quickly), so if you are comparing offers from multiple lenders it must be done on the same day.

For example, if you are shopping mortgage rates and have a quote for a 30 year fixed at 6%, only compare it to other 30 year fixed quotes on the same day. And, be sure to check the costs for the same rate. For example, if the rate is 6%, get the total costs at 6% from each lender. A 6% rate with zero points is very different than 6% and paying 2 "points" (one "point" is one percent of the loan amount). Also, don't forget to ask about other "lender" closing costs. This has become a one of the little tricks of the trade – a lender quotes you a certain rate and zero points, but then has $3,000 – $4,000 in various lender fees (to make up for not charging you points). If you ask only about rate and not the other costs, you may not get the whole picture.

These other fees can be found on the Good Faith Estimate. This, along with any points, is the price of the mortgage. The lender with the lowest combination of costs and rates has the best mortgage rates for you. Of course, also be sure that this lender is a professional who you feel you can trust and develop a lasting relationship. You cannot do this with a call center, for example.

Remember, if you ask for a No/Zero Closing Cost Loan you can get one. Just be aware that you will be paying higher mortgage rates in exchange for it.

Paying higher points and fees will result in lower mortgage rates. For example, at 7.5% you may have zero points and fees, while at 5.5% you may have points and fees of $3000. To get the best mortgage rates, you must estimate how long you will have the mortgage.

Mortgage Tricks to Watch Out For

Mortgage lenders have a reputation for being among the sleaziest, least trustworthy business people in America. Unfortunately, the reputation is deserved in many cases. Please understand, there are plenty of good, smart, and honest mortgage professionals out there. It is your job to find them by asking for referrals from those you trust and doing your homework. Because, the truth is, there are plenty of dishonest mortgage lenders and brokers who will prey on your inexperience.

Here are some of the most common mortgage tricks and scams.

The "Low-Ball" Offer Scam

To get customers in the door, some brokers and lenders will advertise low-ball rates or fees that they have no intention of honoring. Once they get you in the door, they will play "bait and switch," or "let 'em dangle." This is certainly not unique to the mortgage industry – scam artists have been doing this since "selling" was invented. However, it is particularly prevalent in the mortgage industry.

The "Bait and Switch" Scam

Again, this is similar to other dishonest merchants who advertise a great, too-good-to-be-true price, but when you arrive to buy they "happen" to be out of that particular item. But, lucky for you, they "just happen to have this other slightly more expensive" item available.

In the mortgage world, the equivalent is finding that you do not qualify for the price they quoted. Often, the reasons are that your credit score is too low, or the value of your property is too low. TAKE NOTE: it could be entirely possible that this is true if you have not done your homework ahead of time. You MUST know your credit scores and you MUST know the value of what you are seeking to buy. You can do this by checking your credit scores (not just a report, but the actual scores) before you ever shop for a loan, and by working with a qualified buyer's agent who has excellent knowledge of the neighborhood and surrounding area (so they will know values and have comps to back them up). If you are an educated and prepared mortgage buyer, you should not fall prey to a bait and switch.

The "Let 'em Dangle" Scam

There are several variations of this, but essentially, this means that the broker or lender will quote a low- ball rate and then do various things to delay you with all sorts of excuses, all while keeping you excited and "on the hook" while waiting and hoping that rates will drop enough to be able to give you the rate and still make a good profit on the loan. This kind of scam can end up costing you more in a couple of ways: you could end up missing your closing deadlines and either losing deposits or paying extension fees, or you could end up with even higher rates than you could have initially had if rates move higher while you are being "dangled." Bottom line: if you run into delays all of a sudden and sense that you are not getting the full story (some delays are very legitimate – you need to receive a full explanation of what they are and what is being done to solve the issue) or your instincts tell you that something is not right; seek another opinion as quickly as you can.

One good rule of thumb to protect yourself from low-ball type scams is to ignore any ad or quote that is ½ point lower than the other quotes you are seeing. The simple truth is that most lenders have just about the same rates because they all get their money from the same couple sources on Wall Street. Very rarely will a lender be able to offer a significantly different rate than other lenders and still maintain a profitable business. Just remember what you probably were taught as a kid: if it sounds too good to be true, it probably is.

The "Bait and Remember" Scam

This is a classic scam if the mortgage world. The scam happens when the mortgage broker to simply fails to mention certain fees until the loan application is well in process and the borrower is in too deep to bail out. Then, all of a sudden, they "remember" them.

A second version of this is when they give the borrower their Good Faith Estimate with several "estimates" that are ridiculously low (then remind you that they were just estimates). This was very common because brokers knew that mortgage shoppers would ask for a Good Faith Estimate and just compare the bottom line numbers without looking to see if they were reasonable or not. So, the honest broker who fully disclosed the fees was ruled out by the borrower in favor of the lower fees. Then, the dishonest broker "remembers" what the actual fees are and reminds you that all those were just initial estimates. And, the borrower is so deep into the process that they don't have time to switch lenders.

By my estimate, after twenty years of seeing this scam (and others) in action, I would estimate that 70% -80% of brokers and lenders were doing some version of the "Bait and Remember" at one time. No wonder mortgage brokers are trusted less than used car salesmen whenever those polls are taken.

Fortunately there is good news: this scam is now virtually impossible to pull off, thanks to the introduction of a new Good Faith Estimate in 2010. See Chapter 6 for details on the application, including the 2010 Good Faith Estimate.

The "Play the Market" Scam

This is a fairly simple one that can end up costing you money in terms of higher rates or fees, or penalty fees for delayed closings. Typically, there is a lag between the time a borrower submits an application and the time when the loan terms are locked. The lender will likely explain to the borrower that the terms quoted at time of application are subject to change with the market. In fact, it is always in writing in your package of disclosures unless you lock your rate at the time application, which most people do not do.

The scam is simple: if, during this lag time to lock-in or closing (if you have not locked at all), interest rates subsequently rise; the borrower will then see the rate on his loan rise. But, if the going rates decline, on the other hand, dishonest lenders will leave the rate on the loan unchanged and pocket the extra profit (unless the smart borrower challenges it).

Your protection against this is to monitor interest rates during the period from application to locking the loan, and let the loan provider know you are doing so.

The "Pre-Payment Penalty" Scam

Some borrowers will simply accept whatever they are told by their mortgage lender. You must read every single page of your loan disclosures (yes, it is a ton of legalese mumbo-jumbo, but that does not mean to not read it or ask questions on items you do not understand). One common scam that is also now more difficult for lenders to do is to give you a loan with a hidden pre-payment penalty and not tell the borrower about it.

The reason lenders do this is that they make more money on the loan from the Wall Street investors who back loans (having a pre-payment penalty on a loan makes the loan worth more, and therefore lenders are compensated to sell them). For the borrower, you may never even know you had a penalty unless you tried to sell or refinance the house within the penalty period. And, of course, by then the scammer who sold you the loan is long gone and you have documents you signed agreeing to the penalty (in the small print). Your protection is simple: read all your documents, especially your GFE and Truth in Lending disclosure, where it is now clearly disclosed.

While shopping for good rates and terms is important, it is not the only thing. I have lost count how many times I have been called in to fix a problem and save a closing due to someone being taken by a broker promising the lowest rates. If you are only concerned about rates, and choose to ignore service and professionalism, you should <u>do so at your own risk</u>. Then, be prepared for lies, lousy service and wasted time.

The good news is that when you are a well-prepared shopper, you will be able to find a trustworthy professional with whom to work. And, when you work with a trustworthy professional, you will get the best deal for your situation.

Chapter 5
Why You Need a Good Real Estate Agent to Buy Your Home

Buying a home is no small matter. Besides being the largest financial transaction you may ever undertake, it's probably also the most complex. There are many good reasons to work with a qualified real estate professional.

When you work with a good, qualified buyer's agent, your interests become their interests. They are there to protect and serve your interests only – not the seller's.

Additionally, as a first time home buyer, it is understandable that you do not know all the "ins and outs" and tricks of the trade when it comes to buying a home. A trustworthy buyer's agent, along with your mortgage professional, will become your best friend during the home buying process.

Now, here's the bottom-line truth: just like with mortgage lenders, there are more dishonest and unqualified real estate agents than there are smart and trustworthy ones. Shopping for the right professional to work with is just as important as shopping for the home itself.

Don't let this last paragraph scare you too much. There are plenty of great mortgage lenders and real estate agents out there – you just need to do your homework. As I mentioned in the last chapter, this is not a time to be lazy. Buying a home is likely to be the largest financial transaction you have ever made, so you should probably invest the time into finding the right team to help you.

A buyer's representative (or simply buyer's rep) is a licensed real estate professional that represents prospective homebuyers in their property transaction. If you've formalized an agency relationship, typically by signing a buyer's rep agreement (NOTE: do not sigh any buyer's agency agreements until you are 100% sure that you are committed to working with only that person. That most likely means you should not sign anything the first time you meet someone) with a buyer's rep, you can expect him or her to:

- Understand your specific needs and wants, and locate appropriate properties.
- Preview and/or accompany you in viewing properties.
- Research properties, to identify any problems or issues you should consider.
- Advise you in formulating your offer.
- Help you develop your negotiation strategy.
- Provide a list of potential qualified vendors (such as inspectors, attorneys, lenders, etc.) for other related services that may be needed.
- Work closely with your mortgage professional to ensure your closing goes smoothly.
- Keep track of all the other details throughout the entire transaction—to closing and beyond.

In other words, a buyer's rep should make your home buying experience go as smoothly and successfully as possible.

But not all buyers' reps are equal. Choosing the right buyer's agent can be tough. You must choose someone whom you trust and get along with and *like* - not just because you met them at an open house, or because they have a blog, or because they are your sister's husband's friend who is just getting started and needs a break.

Choosing the wrong representation is just not worth it. It will almost certainly cost you time, money and untold stress.

Finding the right buyer's agent is not that difficult. Start by asking friends, neighbors and co-workers, whose opinions you trust, if they had a good experience with an agent and would recommend them. You are likely to hear as many horror stories as good ones, but that is OK, it is all part of the selection process.

If you find a trustworthy, local mortgage professional first, you can also ask them to recommend potential buyer's agents. But, as with any referral, it is still up to you to do your homework.

Take the time to interview your prospective partner – and that is exactly what they are – your partner. Be sure they understand your needs, wants and desires. Remember, they are there to help you so you must communicate clearly with them if the relationship is to work successfully.

Also make sure that they are knowledgeable and experienced in the neighborhoods you are considering. It does you no good to find an otherwise great agent who knows nothing about the town or neighborhood in which you want to shop.

A good buyer's agent will also more-than-likely save you money on your purchase. Because they intimately know the area and what has sold at what prices, they will be invaluable to you when it comes time to formulate your purchase offer.

My advice: take the time to find a qualified buyer's rep. You will be happy you did.

Chapter 6

The Mortgage Application -
A Practical Guide to the 1003

The basic loan application is called the "1003." You will use this application for virtually any mortgage loan. The name "1003" has a very simple origin: the form is form number 1003 as issued by the Federal National Mortgage Association (Fannie Mae).

The application must be completed by anyone who will be on the loan. And, each person must qualify. This means that if you have two people on the application, both must meet the minimum credit standards – one does not "pull up" the other.

If you are married you will have the choice of putting both spouses on the application, or just one. Keep in mind, if you use only one spouse, this means using only that one's income, assets and credit. You cannot pick and choose, such as taking one person's credit and the other's income. It is either all or none. If you choose to put only one spouse on the application, both can still be on the deed to the house, thereby sharing ownership.

On the following pages, each section of the application is broken down and examined in more detail. At first glance the application looks daunting. But when you see how many parts you can leave blank (they will be filled in as the application is completed by the lender), it is not so bad. The important thing to remember is that a good loan professional will be there to help you with anything you do not understand.

The Uniform Residential Loan Application

Page 1, Section 1 – Type of Mortgage and Terms

Uniform Residential Loan Application

This application is designed to be completed by the applicant(s) with the Lender's assistance. Applicants should complete this form as "Borrower" or "Co-Borrower", as applicable. Co-Borrower information must also be provided (and the appropriate box checked) when ☐ the income or assets of a person other than the "Borrower" (including the Borrower's spouse) will be used as a basis for loan qualification or ☐ the income or assets of the Borrower's spouse or other person who has community property rights pursuant to state law will not be used as a basis for loan qualification, but his or her liabilities must be considered because the spouse or other person has community property rights pursuant to applicable law and Borrower resides in a community property state, the security property is located in a community property state, or the Borrower is relying on other property located in a community property state as a basis for repayment of the loan.

If this is an application for joint credit, Borrower and Co-Borrower each agree that we intend to apply for joint credit (sign below).

Borrower _____   Co-Borrower _____

I. TYPE OF MORTGAGE AND TERMS OF LOAN					
Mortgage Applied for: ☐ VA ☐ FHA	☑ Conventional ☐ USDA/Rural Housing Service	☐ Other (explain):		Agency Case Number	Lender Case Number
Amount $	Interest Rate %	No. of Months	Amortization Type: ☑ Fixed Rate ☐ GPM	☐ Other (explain): ☐ ARM (type):	

Section one, on page one, can basically be ignored by you when you fill out the initial application. Your mortgage professional will know which type of loan you are seeking after discussing all of the options with you and can fill this information in as he or she issues the approval. You are not expected to know the rate or terms of your loan when you apply.

However, remember to sign your names above section one.

Page 1, Section 2 – Property & Purpose

II. PROPERTY INFORMATION AND PURPOSE OF LOAN					
Subject Property Address (street, city, state, & ZIP)					No. of Units
Legal Description of Subject Property (attach description if necessary)					Year Built
Purpose of Loan ☑ Purchase ☐ Construction ☐ Refinance ☐ Construction-Permanent ☐ Other (explain):				Property will be: ☑ Primary Residence ☐ Secondary Residence ☐ Investment	
Complete this line if construction or construction-permanent loan.					
Year Lot Acquired	Original Cost $	Amount Existing Liens $	(a) Present Value of Lot $	(b) Cost of Improvements $	Total (a+b) $
Complete this line if this is a refinance loan.					
Year Acquired	Original Cost $	Amount Existing Liens $	Purpose of Refinance	Describe Improvements Cost: $	☐ made ☐ to be made
Title will be held in what Name(s)			Manner in which Title will be held		Estate will be held in: ☑ Fee Simple ☐ Leasehold (show expiration date)
Source of Down Payment, Settlement Charges and/or Subordinate Financing (explain)					

Section two has a couple if important parts to it. If you already have the home under contract, you will need to provide the details here. List the actual address as well as the legal description. Adding the zip code will help, although the form does not ask for it. The "number of units" is usually "1" unless you are buying a duplex or other multi-family home. The "year built" can be ignored for now, as it will be noted on the appraisal.

The purpose of your loan is a "Purchase" if you are buying a home.

Title will be held in your (the borrower and co-borrower) names in most cases. The manner in which the title will be held will either be "individual" or "joint," depending on whether you are doing the loan yourself or with a co-borrower.

Any down payment you make requires you to list the source of the funds. This is typically as simple as "savings."

Page 1, Section 3 – All About You.

Borrower	III. BORROWER INFORMATION	Co-Borrower
Borrower's Name (include Jr. or Sr. if applicable)		Co-Borrower's Name (include Jr. or Sr. if applicable)

Social Security Number	Home Phone (incl. area code)	DOB (mm/dd/yyyy)	Yrs. School	Social Security Number	Home Phone (incl. area code)	DOB (mm/dd/yyyy)	Yrs. School

☐Married ☐Unmarried (include single, ☐Separated divorced, widowed)	Dependents (not listed by Co-Borrower) no. ages	☐Married ☐Unmarried (include single, ☐Separated divorced, widowed)	Dependents (not listed by Borrower) no. ages
Present Address (street, city, state, ZIP) ☐Own ☐Rent ____ No. Yrs.		Present Address (street, city, state, ZIP) ☐Own ☐Rent ____ No. Yrs.	
Mailing Address, if different from Present Address		Mailing Address, if different from Present Address	

If residing at present address for less than two years, complete the following:

Former Address (street, city, state, ZIP) ☐Own ☐Rent ____ No. Yrs.	Former Address (street, city, state, ZIP) ☐Own ☐Rent ____ No. Yrs.
Former Address (street, city, state, ZIP) ☐Own ☐Rent ____ No. Yrs.	Former Address (street, city, state, ZIP) ☐Own ☐Rent ____ No. Yrs.

Fannie Mae Form 1003 07/05
CALYX Form Loanapp1.frm 09/05

Page 1 of 5

Borrower _____
Co-Borrower _____

Freddie Mac Form 65 07/05

Section three is very important. This is where we find out who you are and where you live. Each field in this section needs to be accurately completed. If there is a co-borrower, all information for them is also needed.

Don't forget to initial the bottom of the application on each page.

Page 2, Section 4 – Employment Info

Borrower			IV. EMPLOYMENT INFORMATION	Co-Borrower		
Name & Address of Employer	☐ Self Employed	Yrs. on this job	Name & Address of Employer	☐ Self Employed	Yrs. on this job	
		Yrs. employed in this line of work/profession			Yrs. employed in this line of work/profession	
Position/Title/Type of Business		Business Phone (incl. area code)	Position/Title/Type of Business		Business Phone (incl. area code)	

If employed in current position for less than two years or if currently employed in more than one position, complete the following:

Name & Address of Employer	☐ Self Employed	Dates (from-to)	Name & Address of Employer	☐ Self Employed	Dates (from-to)	
		Monthly Income $			Monthly Income $	
Position/Title/Type of Business		Business Phone (incl. area code)	Position/Title/Type of Business		Business Phone (incl. area code)	
Name & Address of Employer	☐ Self Employed	Dates (from-to)	Name & Address of Employer	☐ Self Employed	Dates (from-to)	
		Monthly Income $			Monthly Income $	
Position/Title/Type of Business		Business Phone (incl. area code)	Position/Title/Type of Business		Business Phone (incl. area code)	
Name & Address of Employer	☐ Self Employed	Dates (from-to)	Name & Address of Employer	☐ Self Employed	Dates (from-to)	
		Monthly Income $			Monthly Income $	
Position/Title/Type of Business		Business Phone (incl. area code)	Position/Title/Type of Business		Business Phone (incl. area code)	
Name & Address of Employer	☐ Self Employed	Dates (from-to)	Name & Address of Employer	☐ Self Employed	Dates (from-to)	
		Monthly Income $			Monthly Income $	
Position/Title/Type of Business		Business Phone (incl. area code)	Position/Title/Type of Business		Business Phone (incl. area code)	

Your employment information is required for at least the last two years. If you are a W-2 employee, your last two years of employment will be verified. If you are self-employed, you will need to provide proof of self-employment, along with two years of tax returns. If you cannot verify your employment or self-employment, you will not likely be approved.

Page 2, Section 5 – Monthly Income and Housing Expense

V. MONTHLY INCOME AND COMBINED HOUSING EXPENSE INFORMATION							
Gross Monthly Income	Borrower	Co-Borrower	Total	Combined Monthly Housing Expense	Present	Proposed	
Base Empl. Income*	$	$	$	Rent	$		
Overtime				First Mortgage (P&I)		$	
Bonuses				Other Financing (P&I)			
Commissions				Hazard Insurance			
Dividends/Interest				Real Estate Taxes			
Net Rental Income				Mortgage Insurance			
Other(before completing, see the notice in "describe other income," below)				Homeowner Assn. Dues			
				Other:			
Total	$	$	$	Total	$	$	

* Self Employed Borrower(s) may be required to provide additional documentation such as tax returns and financial statements.

Describe Other Income   *Notice:* Alimony, child support, or separate maintenance income need not be revealed if the Borrower (B) or Co-Borrower (C) does not choose to have it considered for repaying this loan.

B/C	Monthly Amount
	$

Fannie Mae Form 1003   07/05
CALYX Form Loanapp2.frm 09/05   Page 2 of 5   Borrower _____   Freddie Mac Form 65   07/05
          Co-Borrower _____

Your monthly income should be listed here for both the borrower and co-borrower. Take care to be accurate with your base salary and any overtime or bonuses. If you are inaccurate here, it may cause problems with your approval or cause you to be denied if you have been deceptive.

Overtime and bonuses are treated in a very specific way. You must have a two year history of overtime or bonus income in order to have it count towards your qualifying income. The amount you will be given credit for is the average of the last two years.

If your income is part time, you must have a two year history on that job. The average of your W-2's will be taken to get the qualifying income.

Your current mortgage or rental payment needs to be listed, along with any second mortgage and taxes and insurance you pay monthly. You do not need to complete the "proposed" section, as the lender will complete this once the final loan numbers are ready.

Page 3, Section 6 – Assets and Liabilities

VI. ASSETS AND LIABILITIES					
This Statement and any applicable supporting schedules may be completed jointly by both married and unmarried Co-borrowers if their assets and liabilities are sufficiently joined so that the Statement can be meaningfully and fairly presented on a combined basis; otherwise, separate Statements and Schedules are required. If the Co-Borrower section was completed about a non-applicant spouse or other person, this Statement and supporting schedules must be completed by that spouse or other person also. Completed ☑ Jointly ☐ Not Jointly					
ASSETS Description	Cash or Market Value	Liabilities and Pledged Assets. List the creditor's name, address and account number for all outstanding debts, including automobile loans, revolving charge accounts, real estate loans, alimony, child support, stock pledges, etc. Use continuation sheet, if necessary. Indicate by (*) those liabilities which will be satisfied upon sale of real estate owned or upon refinancing of the subject property.			
Cash deposit toward purchase held by:	$				
		LIABILITIES		Monthly Payment & Months Left to Pay	Unpaid Balance
List checking and savings accounts below		Name and address of Company		$ Payment/Months	$
Name and address of Bank, S&L. or Credit Union					
		Acct. no.			
Acct. no.	$	Name and address of Company		$ Payment/Months	$
Name and address of Bank, S&L. or Credit Union					
		Acct. no.			
Acct. no.	$	Name and address of Company		$ Payment/Months	$
Name and address of Bank, S&L. or Credit Union					
		Acct. no.			
Acct. no	$	Name and address of Company		$ Payment/Months	$
Stocks & Bonds (Company name/number description)	$				
		Acct. no.			
		Name and address of Company		$ Payment/Months	$
Life insurance net cash value	$				
Face amount: $					
Subtotal Liquid Assets	$	Acct. no.			
Real estate owned (enter market value from schedule of real estate owned)	$	Name and address of Company		$ Payment/Months	$
Vested interest in retirement fund	$				
Net worth of business(es) owned (attach financial statement)	$	Acct. no.			
Automobiles owned (make and year)	$	Alimony/Child Support/Separate Maintenance Payments Owed to:		$	
Other Assets (itemize)	$	Job-Related Expense (child care, union dues, etc.)		$	
		Total Monthly Payments		$	
Total Assets a.	$	Net Worth (a minus b) ⇒	$	Total Liabilities b.	$

Accuracy in section six is extremely important. Take the time to list out your savings and assets, and be sure you can back up what you list with actual bank statements. Typically, you will need 60 to 90 days of statements. Lenders will look for any large increases in your balances and question their origin. Be prepared to explain any large increases. If you cannot document where the money came from, it will not be acceptable as assets to the lender. Be sure to discuss any potential issues with your loan professional.

Many borrowers assume the lender will see their liabilities on the credit report, so they ignore the liability section. This is a mistake. Credit reports often contain errors. If you do not list your current liabilities accurately, you run the risk of having an error cause a delay or even a denial on your application. Spend the few minutes it takes and list every current liability accurately.

Page 3, Section 6 part B – Real Estate Owned

The real estate owned section should be completed for all property you currently own. This includes your current residence, any rental properties, and the lot you will be building on, if you own it. As a first time buyer, this section would be left blank.

VII. DETAILS OF TRANSACTION	
a. Purchase price	$
b. Alterations, improvements, repairs	
c. Land (if acquired separately)	
d. Refinance (incl. debts to be paid off)	
e. Estimated prepaid items	
f. Estimated closing costs	
g. PMI, MIP, Funding Fee	
h. Discount (if Borrower will pay)	
i. Total costs (add items a through h)	
j. Subordinate financing	
k. Borrower's closing costs paid by Seller	
l. Other Credits (explain)	
m. Loan amount (exclude PMI, MIP, Funding Fee financed)	
n. PMI, MIP, Funding Fee financed	
o. Loan amount (add m & n)	
p. Cash from/to Borrower (subtract j, k, l & o from i)	

Section seven is simple: ignore it. You are not expected to know the details of your transaction (in lender language). Your lender will complete this section after reviewing your application with you and once the terms are finalized.

VIII. DECLARATIONS

If you answer "Yes" to any questions a through i, please use continuation sheet for explanation.	Borrower		Co-Borrower	
	Yes	No	Yes	No
a. Are there any outstanding judgments against you?	☐	☐	☐	☐
b. Have you been declared bankrupt within the past 7 years?	☐	☐	☐	☐
c. Have you had property foreclosed upon or given title or deed in lieu thereof in the last 7 years?	☐	☐	☐	☐
d. Are you a party to a lawsuit?	☐	☐	☐	☐
e. Have you directly or indirectly been obligated on any loan which resulted in foreclosure, transfer of title in lieu of foreclosure, or judgment? (This would include such loans as home mortgage loans, SBA loans, home improvement loans, educational loans, manufactured (mobile) home loans, any mortgage, financial obligation, bond, or loan guarantee. If "Yes," provide details, including date, name and address of Lender, FHA or VA case number, if any, and reasons for the action.)	☐	☐	☐	☐
f. Are you presently delinquent or in default on any Federal debt or any other loan, mortgage, financial obligation, bond, or loan guarantee? If "Yes," give details as described in the preceding question.	☐	☐	☐	☐
g. Are you obligated to pay alimony, child support, or separate maintenance?	☐	☐	☐	☐
h. Is any part of the down payment borrowed?	☐	☐	☐	☐
i. Are you a co-maker or endorser on a note?	☐	☐	☐	☐
j. Are you a U. S. citizen?	☐	☐	☐	☐
k. Are you a permanent resident alien?	☐	☐	☐	☐
l. Do you intend to occupy the property as your primary residence? If "Yes," complete question m below.	☐	☐	☐	☐
m. Have you had an ownership interest in a property in the last three years?	☐	☐	☐	☐
(1) What type of property did you own-principal residence (PR), second home (SH), or investment property (IP)?	____		____	
(2) How did you hold title to the home-solely by yourself (S), jointly with your spouse (SP), or jointly with another person (O)?	____		____	

Unlike section seven, section eight is important and needs to be completed in full. You must honestly answer each question for both the borrower and co-borrower. Failure to do so could result in a denial.

Page 4, Section 9 - Signature

IX. ACKNOWLEDGEMENT AND AGREEMENT

Each of the undersigned specifically represents to Lender and to Lender's actual or potential agents, brokers, processors, attorneys, insurers, servicers, successors and assigns and agrees and acknowledges that: (1) the information provided in this application is true and correct as of the date set forth opposite my signature and that any intentional or negligent misrepresentation of this information contained in this application may result in civil liability, including monetary damages, to any person who may suffer any loss due to reliance upon any misrepresentation that I have made on this application, and/or in criminal penalties including, but not limited to, fine or imprisonment or both under the provisions of Title 18, United States Code, Sec. 1001, et seq.; (2) the loan requested pursuant to this application (the "Loan") will be secured by a mortgage or deed of trust on the property described in this application; (3) the property will not be used for any illegal or prohibited purpose or use; (4) all statements made in this application are made for the purpose of obtaining a residential mortgage loan; (5) the property will be occupied as indicated in this application; (6) the Lender, its servicers, successors or assigns may retain the original and/or an electronic record of this application, whether or not the Loan is approved; (7) the Lender and its agents, brokers, insurers, servicers, successors and assigns may continuously rely on the information contained in the application, and I am obligated to amend and/or supplement the information provided in this application if any of the material facts that I have represented herein should change prior to closing of the Loan; (8) in the event that my payments on the Loan become delinquent, the Lender, its servicers, successors or assigns may, in addition to any other rights and remedies that it may have relating to such delinquency, report my name and account information to one or more consumer reporting agencies; (9) ownership of the Loan and/or administration of the Loan account may be transferred with such notice as may be required by law; (10) neither Lender nor its agents, brokers, insurers, servicers, successors or assigns has made any representation or warranty, express or implied, to me regarding the property or the condition or value of the property; and (11) my transmission of this application as an "electronic record" containing my "electronic signature," as those terms are defined in applicable federal and/or state laws (excluding audio and video recordings), or my facsimile transmission of this application containing a facsimile of my signature, shall be as effective, enforceable and valid as if a paper version of this application were delivered containing my original written signature.

Acknowledgement. Each of the undersigned hereby acknowledges that any owner of the Loan, its servicers, successors and assigns, may verify or reverify any information contained in this application or obtain any information or data relating to the Loan, for any legitimate purpose through any source, including a source named in this application or a consumer reporting agency.

Borrower's Signature	Date	Co-Borrower's Signature	Date
X		X	

Section nine is simply your signature. You are certifying that the information you supplied is truthful and accurate.

Page 4, Section 10 – Government Monitoring

X. INFORMATION FOR GOVERNMENT MONITORING PURPOSES

The following information is requested by the Federal Government for certain types of loans related to a dwelling in order to monitor the lender's compliance with equal credit opportunity, fair housing and home mortgage disclosure laws. You are not required to furnish this information, but are encouraged to do so. The law provides that a Lender may not discriminate either on the basis of this information, or on whether you choose to furnish it. If you furnish the information, please provide both ethnicity and race. For race, you may check more than one designation. If you do not furnish ethnicity, race, or sex, under Federal regulations this lender is required to note the information on the basis of visual observation and surname if you have made this application in person. If you do not wish to furnish the information, please check the box below. (Lender must review the above material to assure that the disclosures satisfy all requirements to which the lender is subject under applicable state law for the particular type of loan applied for.)

BORROWER ☐ I do not wish to furnish this information			CO-BORROWER ☐ I do not wish to furnish this information		
Ethnicity: ☐ Hispanic or Latino	☐ Not Hispanic or Latino		Ethnicity: ☐ Hispanic or Latino	☐ Not Hispanic or Latino	
Race: ☐ American Indian or Alaska Native	☐ Asian	☐ Black or African American	Race: ☐ American Indian or Alaska Native	☐ Asian	☐ Black or African American
☐ Native Hawaiian or Other Pacific Islander	☐ White		☐ Native Hawaiian or Other Pacific Islander	☐ White	
Sex: ☐ Female	☐ Male		Sex: ☐ Female	☐ Male	
To be Completed by Interviewer This application was taken by:	Interviewer's Name (print or type)		Name and Address of Interviewer's Employer		
☐ Face-to-face interview ☐ Mail	Interviewer's Signature	Date			
☐ Telephone ☐ Internet	Interviewer's Phone Number (incl. area code)				

Fannie Mae Form 1003 07/05
CALYX Form Loanapp4.frm 09/05

Page 4 of 5

Freddie Mac Form 65 07/05

The borrower is asked to disclose his or her ethnicity, race and sex so the government can monitor compliance with the Fair Credit Act and other anti-discrimination laws. You, as the borrower, have the option of declining to provide this information and you cannot be penalized for doing so. The choice is yours and it will not affect your application or approval.

The final page of the 1003 is blank and is used as a continuation page for any sections that may need more space. Use this page for any additional information you may need to provide, or leave it blank.

There you have it – the entire loan application simplified and reduced to only what you really need to know. Be sure to consult with your loan professional if you have any questions when it comes time to complete your application.

The 2010 GFE (Good Faith Estimate)

A big change occurred in the mortgage world on January 1, 2010. On that date, HUD changed the entire look and (more importantly) importance of the Good Faith Estimate form (the "GFE"). This is important no matter how large or small your loan is, because you need to know exactly how much your mortgage is going to cost. This means knowing not just the interest rate, but all the fees and charges you'll have to pay to close the loan. Until the new GFE went into effect, Good Faith Estimates were one of the biggest sources of fraud in the mortgage industry. This new form, and the requirements attached to it, provides a much more accurate snapshot of the entire costs of your loan.

Until this point HUD had generally allowed lenders to offer their own Good Faith Estimate of Closing Costs. Now, this new standard form that all lenders must use finally assures that borrowers actually understand what's being charged for their loans, why and by whom.

"The mortgage crisis," says former HUD Secretary Steve Preston, the last HUD secretary appointed by President Bush, "was fueled in part by people agreeing to mortgages that they ultimately could not afford. In some cases, people didn't understand or know that their mortgages could result in large payment increases after just two or three years. Others did not recognize the total costs that come with homeownership. And others paid higher loan origination and closing costs simply because they did not know about other affordable options."

So what makes this form better?

First, it's a three-page document that every lender must use. This means that you can compare all offers from all lenders and know that you are getting an "apples to apples" comparison. This was virtually impossible before this form came into existence.

Second, the document is not just a list of fees and charges, it also explains in basic terms the purpose of each expense.

Third, lenders will have to show their yield-spread premiums (YSPs), costs which were rarely understood by, or fully disclosed to, borrowers. HUD finally realized that these premiums are directly tied to the higher interest rates that borrowers pay.

Reading the New GFE Form

Page One:

The first page is actually a summary of loan costs, while the specifics are found on page two.

The first section to know is the Important Dates section. Lines 1 and 2 tell you how long the quoted rate and terms last. Items 3 and 4 concern loan lock-ins and how long the rates and terms will last if you lock them in at the time the GFE is issued.

The Summary of Your Loan section tells you the amount of the loan, the initial loan rate and monthly payment.

IMPORTANT: If you have an adjustable rate mortgage (an "ARM"), the next few items will tell you:

- How high the interest rate can go.
- When the interest rate can first rise.
- The maximum monthly payment you can expect.
- If a prepayment penalty is allowed and, if yes, how much it will cost.
- Whether there is a balloon payment at the end of the loan terms.

Next the form will tell you whether the lender will create an escrow or "trust" account to collect money each month for property taxes and insurance. In nearly every instance, if you buy with less than 20 percent down, an escrow account is required by the lender. This is not negotiable.

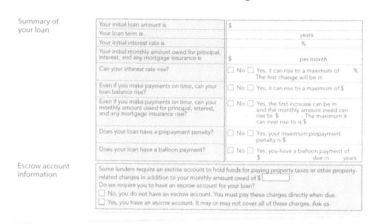

Finally, the form adds your origination charges (the "A" items on page two) with other settlement costs (the "B" items on page two). Be aware that you can have additional costs at closing, depending on how the sale agreement is written.

Good Faith Estimate (HUD-GFE) 1

Page Two:

The second page is divided into two parts, A and B. Part A looks at "origination" fees, the cost to buy your mortgage.

First, the form shows your origination fee in a dollar amount, including any yield spread premium (YSP). Under the old rules, the yield spread premium could be shown as either a dollar amount or as a percentage of the loan. Now, the entire cost of the loan, including any YSP, is shown as a single dollar amount.

Next, the form shows if your interest rate is being impacted by the origination fee. In other words, let's say you can borrow $100,000 at 6 percent interest over 30 years with no points. This is called the par pricing for this loan. But, let's say that you could also borrow $100,000 at 5.75 percent — if you were willing to pay 1 point at closing. A point is equal to 1 percent of the loan amount or $1,000 in this case. The form shows if you are paying for any reduction of the interest rate OR any increase in the rate by paying a smaller origination fee.

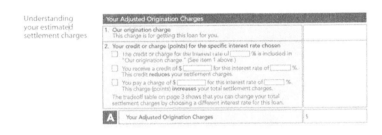

Next we go to part B. This part of the form shows the cash costs you can expect to pay at settlement (or escrow) when the loan closes. As the bottom of part B is a total which shows "Your Charges for All Other Settlement Services."

The totals for parts A and B are then shown at the bottom of the page and on the bottom of page one as well.

	Your Charges for All Other Settlement Services
Some of these charges can change at settlement. See the top of page 3 for more information.	**3. Required services that we select** These charges are for services we require to complete your settlement. We will choose the providers of these services. Service _____ Charge _____
	4. Title services and lender's title insurance This charge includes the services of a title or settlement agent, for example, and title insurance to protect the lender, if required.
	5. Owner's title insurance You may purchase an owner's title insurance policy to protect your interest in the property.
	6. Required services that you can shop for These charges are for other services that are required to complete your settlement. We can identify providers of these services or you can shop for them yourself. Our estimates for providing these services are below. Service _____ Charge _____
	7. Government recording charges These charges are for state and local fees to record your loan and title documents.
	8. Transfer taxes These charges are for state and local fees on mortgages and home sales.
	9. Initial deposit for your escrow account This charge is held in an escrow account to pay future recurring charges on your property and includes ☐ all property taxes, ☐ all insurance, and ☐ other _____ .
	10. Daily interest charges This charge is for the daily interest on your loan from the day of your settlement until the first day of the next month or the first day of your normal mortgage payment cycle. This amount is $_____ per day for _____ days (if your settlement is _____).
	11. Homeowner's insurance This charge is for the insurance you must buy for the property to protect from a loss, such as fire. Policy _____ Charge _____

B	Your Charges for All Other Settlement Services	$
A + **B**	Total Estimated Settlement Charges	$

 Good Faith Estimate (HUD-GFE) 2

Page Three:

The last page should really be the first page because it contains instructions for understanding the form.

The first section lists charges that the lender cannot increase, charges that can rise by as much as 10 percent, and charges that change prior to settlement. This is important information; it means that you should check the numbers on your good faith estimate with the final figures presented to you at closing.

Understanding which charges can change at settlement

This GFE estimates your settlement charges. At your settlement, you will receive a HUD-1, a form that lists your actual costs. Compare the charges on the HUD-1 with the charges on this GFE. Charges can change if you select your own provider and do not use the companies we identify. (See below for details.)

These charges cannot increase at settlement	The total of these charges can increase up to 10% at settlement	These charges can change at settlement
• Our origination charge • Your credit or charge (points) for the specific interest rate chosen (after you lock in your interest rate) • Your adjusted origination charge (after you lock in your interest rate) • Transfer taxes	• Required services that we select • Title services and lender's title insurance (if we select them or you use companies we identify) • Owner's title insurance (if you use companies we identify) • Required services that you can shop for (if you use companies we identify) • Government recording charges	• Required services that you can shop for (if you do not use companies we identify) • Title services and lender's title insurance (if you do not use companies we identify) • Owner's title insurance (if you do not use companies we identify) • Initial deposit for your escrow account • Daily interest charges • Homeowner's Insurance

Next, HUD gets into the issue of higher or lower settlement fees. In the same way that mortgage loans have par pricing, so does the settlement process. In other words, if you are willing to pay a somewhat higher interest rate you may be able to lower your cash costs at closing. Indeed, you may not have to bring any cash to closing.

Using the tradeoff table

In this GFE, we offered you this loan with a particular interest rate and estimated settlement charges. However:

- If you want to choose this same loan with **lower settlement charges**, then you will have a **higher interest rate**.
- If you want to choose this same loan with a **lower interest rate**, then you will have **higher settlement charges**.

If you would like to choose an available option, you must ask us for a new GFE.

Loan originators have the option to complete this table. Please ask for additional information if the table is not completed.

	The loan in this GFE	The same loan with lower settlement charges	The same loan with a lower interest rate
Your initial loan amount	$	$	$
Your initial interest rate	%	%	%
Your initial monthly amount owed	$	$	$
Change in the monthly amount owed from this GFE	No change	You will pay $ more every month	You will pay $ less every month
Change in the amount you will pay at settlement with this interest rate	No change	Your settlement charges will be **reduced by** $	Your settlement charges will **increase by** $
How much your total estimated settlement charges will be	$	$	$

For an adjustable rate loan, the comparisons above are for the initial interest rate before adjustments are made.

In the third section HUD offers borrowers the opportunity to compare loan offers from different lenders. This is important because borrowers should look at different loan offers to find the rates and terms which best meet your needs.

Use this chart to compare GFEs from different loan originators. Fill in the information by using a different column for each GFE you receive. By comparing loan offers, you can shop for the best loan

	This loan	Loan 2	Loan 3	Loan 4
Loan originator name				
Initial loan amount				
Loan term				
Initial interest rate				
Initial monthly amount owed				
Rate lock period				
Can interest rate rise?				
Can loan balance rise?				
Can monthly amount owed rise?				
Prepayment penalty?				
Balloon payment?				
Total Estimated Settlement Charges				

If your loan is
sold in the future

Some lenders may sell your loan after settlement. Any fees lenders receive in the future cannot change the loan you receive or the charges you paid at settlement

 Good Faith Estimate (HUD-GFE) 3

Lastly, HUD notes that your loan may be sold in the future. If so, after settlement "any fees lenders receive in the future cannot change the loan you receive or the charges you paid at settlement." Translation: A contract is a contract.

The Truth in Lending Disclosure Statement

A Truth in Lending disclosure statement is one of the more important documents in the mortgage process. It is designed to help borrowers understand their borrowing costs in their entirety. Federal law requires that lenders provide a Truth in Lending (TIL) document to all loan applicants within three business days of receiving a loan application, disclosing all costs associated with making and closing the loan.

Here is a breakdown of the some of the charges you may find on your Truth in Lending statement and what they mean:

Annual percentage rate:

The annual percentage rate (APR) is the "cost of credit" or the amount you will pay for the credit provided to you through the loan. APR is calculated at a yearly rate. It includes not only your contractual interest rate, but also any prepaid finance charges paid during or before the loan's closing – such as origination points, service fees or credit fees, commitment or discount fees, buyer's points, finder's feels, etc. – as well as any private mortgage insurance (PMI). PMI is generally required if you put less than 20 percent down on a home. Note that the APR shown on the TIL disclosure statement always exceeds the quoted interest rate because of the additional items noted above. In essence the APR reflects the true cost of your loan.

Finance charge

The finance charge also calculates the cost of credit, however this figure is expressed in dollars rather than a percentage. Like the APR, the finance charge includes the total amount of interest incurred over the loan's lifetime, plus any prepaid finance charges and mortgage insurance premiums.

Amount financed

The amount financed represents the loan amount minus any prepaid finance charges. The amount financed is important because it provides you with a clear, accurate assessment of the total amount of credit provided through the loan.

Total of payments

The total of payments indicates the total amount you will pay over the course of the loan if you make all required payments. This includes the principal, interest and private mortgage insurance (if required), but not your real estate tax premiums or monthly property insurance payments.

Payment schedule

The payment schedule includes the following information: number of payments, amount of payments, and when payments are due. Keep in mind that the amount of payments does not include payments for real estate taxes or property insurance premiums. If you have an Adjustable Rate Mortgage, the payment schedule will reflect the payments due based on any adjustments. If you have mortgage insurance, the payments may be reflected as well.

Other disclosures

Your Truth in Lending statement will contain a number of additional disclosures below the payment schedule information. Some of these may include whether or not your loan has a demand feature and/or a variable rate feature. A demand feature allows the lender to demand payment of the loan for any reason. A variable rate feature means that your interest rate is not fixed and may change. This essentially indicates that you have an adjustable rate mortgage. There is also a section on the Truth in Lending statement that details the late charge terms. This line will tell you when you will be charged a late fee and how much that fee will be.

Another important disclosure to look for is called prepayment. There are two lines under prepayment. The first tells you whether or not you have to pay a penalty if you pay your loan off early. (Remember this fee could apply if you chose to refinance your mortgage or sell your home before the end of your loan term.) The second line states that if you pay the loan off early, you are, unfortunately, not entitled to a refund of part of your finance charge. Basically, this means that you will pay interest for the period of time in which you use the loan and any previously paid finance charges are non-refundable.

Buying a home is a huge decision. If you have any questions about your Truth in Lending disclosure statement, be sure to ask our lender.

Chapter 7
Who is Involved in the Loan Application Process?

There are several people that will be involved with your loan application, in addition to the loan professional with whom you choose to work. Here is a brief summary of each person and their job description. All of these people working together are needed to get you from application to closing in a timely and stress-free manner.

You and Your Family. As important as the mortgage and real estate professionals are to your application; you and your family almost completely dictate the pace and direction of the application process. As the borrower, you are completely in charge and ultimately responsible for your home purchase's success or failure.

The Buyer's Agent. As we have discussed previously, a good buyer's agent is an invaluable member of your team. He or she will be your advocate throughout the process.

The Listing Agent. Just as the buyer's agent is important to you, the buyer, the selling (or "seller's") agent is the advocate for the seller. Typically, the buyer's agent and listing agent will work together to insure a smooth closing.

Behind the Scenes

The Processor. The loan processor works for the lender and will often be your primary point of contact for all items related to documenting your loan application. The processor will collect any and all required documents and package the loan file for submission to the underwriter.

Typically, the processor and the loan officer work together on the file to insure that the loan closes properly and in a timely manner. It is good advice to learn the name if your processor and develop a good working relationship with him or her. This will help the process go more smoothly for you. It is also helpful to understand that the processor is not the underwriter and does not make decisions about your approval. These are handled by the underwriter.

The Underwriter. As discussed earlier, the underwriter is the person who makes the final decision on your loan approval once all of the documentation is complete. Many lenders now use a computer based underwriting system to issue a pre-approval, but there is always a human to review and verify the documentation as the last step of the process.

The underwriter's main job is to review and verify the submitted documentation and compare it to the loan program's guidelines. If everything fits and is in order, the underwriting process is a quick and painless affair. If the documentation is questionable or does not exactly fit the guidelines, underwriting can take longer and require additional paperwork. This can cause delays in your closing or even a denial.

The best approach is to be sure you are able to fully document everything you state on the application. Do not try to "fudge" things, exaggerate your qualifications, or attempt to qualify for more than you can really afford. Most of the problems we see in underwriting come from these three issues.

Remember, the underwriter is your friend, not an enemy. As long as you and your property are qualified for the requested loan, there should never be any problems.

For most lenders, you should allow 3-5 business days for the underwriting process, plus additional time to collect and review any "conditions" they may request. The conditions could be as simple as clarifying something on the application or other paperwork or updating a bank statement or pay stub. They can also be as complicated as requesting additional comps from the appraiser or requiring more documentation to support something on the application. The time line to "clear conditions" will entirely depend on what is requested and how quickly these items can be obtained. This is often where some borrowers get frustrated, mainly because they do not understand the request. It is best to review the conditions immediately with your loan professional so you understand how quickly or easily these items can or cannot be obtained.

Once the loan receives final underwriting approval, your loan will move from the underwriter to the lender's closing department. There, the loan's documents will be prepared and sent to your closing agent for you to sign and "close."

The Appraiser. The appraiser has the job of examining your soon-to-be new home to determine the value for the purpose of the loan.

The appraiser, who is licensed by the state, must follow certain rules regarding how an appraisal is conducted. They must locate similar homes within a close proximity to your location (usually 1-3 miles in most cases) and they must also be on similar size land. This is called finding a "comparable," or "comps." A "comp" is not a "comp" if the home has not sold on the open market within the last six months.

This means if you are buying a 2000 square foot colonial style home on 1/2 acre in a suburban setting, the appraiser must find at least three other roughly 2000 foot (usually within 15% of the size) homes on roughly 1/2 acre of land within a mile or so of your home. If they cannot do this, there are often problems with establishing value. This could lead to a loan denial or to the lender making adjustments to the value (usually lower).

The best advice is to know the area in which you are buying (a good reason to have a qualified buyer's agent on your team) and not try to buy a home that is way out of the ordinary for the area.

The other area of concern for appraisals is the location of the property. The home will be considered to be either in an urban, suburban or rural setting. This will determine how far away the comps can be. Typically, in an urban setting, comps must be a half mile or less from the subject. This may be stretched to a mile in some cases. For suburban properties, one to three miles is the maximum distance allowed in most cases. For rural properties, the comps should be no more than three to five miles away.

There are exceptions to these rules, but you should not count on an exception being made. It is best to understand how an appraisal interacts with your loan application and do as much research as you can before you make any financial commitments.

Appraisal standards became much more stringent in 2009. As of May 1, 2009, Congress passed the Home Valuation Code of Conduct. Essentially, this new law requires all appraisals to be a handled through 3rd party management companies so that lenders, their reps, buyers or sellers are not able to influence the outcome of the valuation. Although this sounds good in theory, the negative is that all appraisals have gotten more expensive (since a middleman has been added) and they now take considerably longer to do than before.

The Closing Agent. The closing agent is the person or company that will actually assist you with the signing of all the documents. This is typically an attorney or a title company. Generally, you can freely choose between either of these to do the closing for you. A few states, however, require you to use an attorney for the closing. Ask your loan professional if you are not sure about your state.

Once your closing agent receives the files from the lender, he or she will need to prepare the documents, which include; among other documents, the note, the deed and the closing statement (called a "HUD-1" most of the time). This usually takes the closing agent a day to do all of this, so schedule accordingly with them.

The fees for closing agents vary around the country and are usually pretty consistent from one to another within a particular market area. Nearly all lenders will allow you to choose your own closing agent, so it is advisable to check around and get an estimate of the costs. These costs are NOT controlled by the lender, so you are free to find the best deal for you. The other fees associated with the closing agent, in addition to the actual cost of document preparation and signing are typically: title insurance, date downs, recording fees, state taxes or assessments, and any courier fees required. Most of the fees on this list are set by the state and the locality, so there is not much shopping around that can be done. It just needs to be accepted part of the cost of buying a home.

There are a couple of other players who are integral in getting your loan closed, although you will not necessarily see them at the closing.

The Insurance Agent. You will need insurance in place prior to closing your new loan. You will need a new homeowner's insurance policy. Typically, you will need to provide a binder for the policy from your agent and a receipt showing that you have paid for the policy.

The Home Inspector. We will discuss home inspectors and their importance in Chapter 16.

Chapter 8

The 4 Essential Ingredients Required for an "Approved" Stamp on your Loan Application.

There are many things that factor into a loan approval. Especially today, if you cannot prove your income and that you can afford to pay for the home you want, you will have trouble finding a lender. It is imperative that you are well-prepared and have all of your documents ready.

Below are 4 essential ingredients that every borrower must have in today's market.

1) Be Aware of Your Credit Situation

Especially in today's lending climate, you must fully understand your credit profile and know your scores. Credit scores that qualified just a year or two ago no longer do now in many cases. Many loan programs now have minimum score requirements of 680 or 720. And to get the very best rates you are hearing about, be prepared to need no less than a 720 to 740 score.

Do not assume your credit is "fine." Just because you qualified for a good car loan does not mean you will get the best mortgage loan.

The best thing to do is check your credit before you even begin the shopping process. Be sure to use a reputable source for credit reports that provides you with a "tri-merge" report with your scores. Free credit reports do not do this, so be prepared to pay about $40. This is money well spent.

2) Be Proactive in the Process

Those who take charge of their situation (this is good advice for anything in life, not just getting a mortgage) will end up having a better experience than those who sit back and expect things to get done for them.

A couple of areas to be sure to stay on top of: 1) follow up and respond in a timely manner with your mortgage professional and your Realtor; 2) Order your home inspection right away; 3) contact your insurance agent to get your policy in place early in the process.

3) Be Realistic

Nothing is worse than falling in love with a certain house, only to find out you cannot afford to buy it. Have a clear understanding of how much you can afford, how much you can qualify for, and how much you are comfortable paying towards your mortgage (both down payment and monthly payment).

While it is a good idea to start with a helpful mortgage calculator; nothing replaces a good, old fashioned consultation with a mortgage professional. He or she will be glad to fully pre-approve you so that you know exactly the price range to shop in and which homes to avoid.

4) Be Prepared.

Have all of your documentation organized before you apply.

You will need to have the following information for your mortgage application in order to expedite the processing of your mortgage loan.

- A check for your appraisal.
- Your residence addresses for the past two years.
- Names, addresses and phone number of your landlords for the past two years.
- Present value of all real estate owned.
- Names, addresses, phone numbers and contact person for all employers for the last two years.
- W-2 Forms for all employers for the last two years.
- Pay stubs covering the most recent 30 day period (all current jobs).
- Addresses, account numbers and current balances for all checking, savings and other deposit accounts.
- Three most recent months' bank statements (all accounts, all pages).
- Name, account numbers, balances and monthly payments for all consumer debt accounts including auto loans, personal loans, student loans, credit union loans and mortgages.
- Name, account numbers, balances and monthly payments for all credit cards used in the last several months.
- Evidence of alimony or child support, a copy of the court order and ages of children.
- Copy of divorce decree and separation agreement.

- Social security and other benefit award letters if being used toward qualifying income.
- Stock information including names of stocks, share owned, current price per share and last three month's stock statements (or most recent quarterly statement).
- Documentation relating to any special issues such as bankruptcy, credit problems and recently established accounts for deposits or loans.

FOR VA LOANS:

- DD214 of Certificate of Eligibility (original)

IF YOU ARE SELF EMPLOYED:

- Two years personal tax returns
- Two years partnership/corporate tax returns (if applicable)
- Sometimes needed: year to date profit and loss statement, signed by accountant

BE SURE YOUR REAL ESTATE AGENT PROVIDES:

- Copy of listing card
- Complete ratified contract of sale (all pages)
- Their personal business card
- Name, address and phone number of condominium management company (if applicable)

Chapter 9
Things You Should NOT Do When
Applying For A Home Loan

In Chapter 8, we discussed four things to do to help insure a smooth loan process. It is also to know what NOT to do, as well as what to do.

Here is a list of things to avoid when you are seeking to obtain financing for a home. The following things can cause an otherwise good application to get denied.

Don't buy or lease an auto before you apply for a mortgage! Lenders look carefully at your debt-to-income ratio. A large payment such as a car lease or purchase can greatly impact those ratios and prevent you from qualifying for a home loan.

Don't move assets from one bank account to another! These transfers show up as new deposits and complicate the application process, as you must then disclose and document the source of funds for each new account. The lender can verify each account as it currently exists. You can consolidate your accounts later if you need to.

Don't change jobs! A new job may involve a probation period, which must be satisfied before income from the new job can be considered for qualifying purposes. If you are considering changing jobs, please be sure to discuss this with your mortgage professional before you make the change.

Don't buy new furniture or major appliances for your new home! It is easy to get excited about your new home. But, remember, it is not your new home until all the documents have been signed, sealed and delivered. If the new purchases increase the amount of debt you are responsible for on a monthly basis, there is the possibility this may disqualify you from getting the loan, or cut down on the available funds you need to meet closing costs.

Don't allow multiple lenders to run your credit. There is actually no reason to have your credit run more than one time during the mortgage shopping process – and that is after you have chosen who to work with. Multiple inquires created in a short time frame from the same lender type (such as from shopping for a mortgage) will not harm your score. But, if they are spread over a longer time (if you shop around for a while), they can hurt your credit scores and potentially cause trouble with your approval.

The best thing to do is run your credit yourself BEFORE you start the process so that you know exactly what your scores are. Then, you can tell the lenders who you are talking to what your scores are so that they don't have to run your credit. If a potential lender tells you they need to run your credit before they can answer your questions, you should immediately move on to a more professional lender. But, remember, you must be accurate in what you tell your lender at this stage to ensure that you get accurate information back from them.

Don't attempt to consolidate bills before speaking with your lender! A good lender can advise you if this needs to be done.

If you are moving, don't pack or ship information needed for the loan application! Important paperwork such as W-2 forms, divorce decrees, and tax returns should not be sent with your household goods. Duplicate copies take weeks to obtain, and could stall the closing date on your transaction.

Don't wait until the last minute to seek a mortgage. If you are purchasing a home, it is wise to get a full pre-approval before you ever look at your first house. Too often, buyers will find a house they love, sign a contract, make a deposit, then start the loan process. Then, they find out there is an issue with the approval or a delay of some kind. Be smart, get the financial side of things sorted out first, and then enjoy the new home shopping process.

Chapter 10
Options for Buying a Home
with As Little as $100 Down (or Less)

Many people think that low-down payment financing is a thing of the past. But mortgage insiders know better! There are still several unique programs that allow any buyer to purchase with little or no money down.

$100 Down. Yes, $100 Down!

This $100 down program is not limited to first time buyers or restricted incomes. It allows buyers to buy homes from a select list of properties in your area. You can participate one of two ways - purchase a "move in ready" home or buy and renovate a home. Either way, you can own a home for as little as $100 down.

Who Offers This Program?

When a FHA (Federal Housing Administration) loan goes to foreclosure and is taken back by FHA, they are in a hurry to sell that property. Just like every lender, FHA is not in the business of owning and selling homes. Since FHA wants to sell these homes as soon as they can, FHA offers specials to buyers to sell these homes faster. One way of doing this is to offer buyer a $100 down loan to buy one of the homes that they are selling. The FHA $100 loan program is available only on homes FHA currently owns. Many buyers who qualify for a traditional FHA loan choose to take advantage of FHA's offer of only putting a down payment of $100 on their owned homes. This is a huge advantage FHA has over other programs.

This program is available in all 50 states and is not limited to first-time buyers, but is an ideal program for first timers who don't have the cash for a traditional down payment.

The best part is - you can buy a home and move right in. Or, if the house isn't perfect; and you want to make some improvements (large or small), you can roll the costs of the renovation right into your new loan. All still for $100 down!

Please note: it is absolutely a must to find a lender that can offer this program. Many lenders have never even heard of this program, and even fewer are able to offer it. Another tip: get pre-approved for this loan AND to work with an Agent who understands this program and how to submit the offer to the seller.

Zero Down Payment: USDA 100% Loans

The USDA Rural Development program supplies $16 billion in funding to Americans in rural areas. Because millions of people qualify for different types of USDA loans, more families are turning to USDA Loans as a lending solution.

One of the benefits available with USDA Home Loans is no down payment on your home. Most people in rural areas qualify for USDA loan benefits, but people living on the outskirts of a city or in a medium sized town may also qualify. In fact, USDA says that over 70% of the nation is covered by this program. You can visit the USDA Home Loan website and enter the property address to see if it is eligible for this program.

USDA Loan Guidelines

Some of the eligibility standards that determine if you qualify for a USDA loan for your home include your income, your credit, what county and zip code the home resides in, as well as the number of dependents you can claim. Because these guidelines are very specific, it is important to work with a mortgage professional that has experience dealing with USDA government financing. This is one of the few remaining loan options that allow no down payment and is an excellent way to buy a home.

The USDA Loan program helps ensure that individuals of the rural communities can compete in the global economy. By allowing communities to obtain these loans they can put into place better community centers, facilities and thus be a place where individuals will relocate and not be hampered by moving to a community that has not been able to update the public facilities. There is over $86 billion in the USDA portfolio of loans and they provide approximately $16 billion annually in program loans, grants, and USDA rural development program loans.

Zero Down Payment: VA Loans

VA's Home Loan Program is for veterans and active duty military personnel and certain members of the reserves and National Guard. VA's program provides an excellent product and benefit for those individuals who have served or are serving to protect our families and our nation, as well as giving them a form of financing that will allow real estate professionals to sell more homes.

For those who are unfamiliar with the program, there are several advantages to using VA's Home Loan Program. The VA allows a veteran who qualifies income and credit-wise to purchase a primary residence without putting money down towards the sales price, as long as the sales price does not exceed the appraised value. Veterans do, however, need money towards closing costs and the earnest money deposit, which the seller generally requires when a sales contract is signed. Closing costs may be paid by the seller, which is an item to consider when the sales price is being negotiated.

Other benefits of using VA's program (other than the 100% financing of the sales price) include:

- Loans are assumable, provided the person assuming the loan is qualified.
- Veterans' closing costs are limited by VA.
- Additional assistance is offered by VA should veterans have problems making their home loan payments in the future.
- Prepayment of the loan without a penalty.
- There is no Private Mortgage Insurance
- Veterans must meet credit standards but loans are not "score driven"

Here are some additional facts about VA purchase transactions:

- VA does not have a maximum loan amount. However, lenders do sell loans on the secondary mortgage market, so they will generally limit loans to the VA limit for the county where the property is located. With a down payment, loans may exceed these amounts.
- The veteran does have to qualify income and credit wise.

- The veteran does have to occupy the home as their primary residence.
- The veteran does not have to be a first time home buyer and may reuse his/her benefit.
- The lender, not VA, sets the interest rate and discount points, so they may vary from lender to lender.
- There is no private mortgage insurance, but VA does charge an upfront VA funding fee, which may be financed. The exception to this is that if a veteran is in receipt of VA service connect disability payments each month, he or she does not have to pay a VA funding fee.
- The seller can pay for closing costs. There is a requirement that seller concessions do not exceed 4%, but only certain items are considered as part of the concession; i.e., payment of pre-paids, VA funding fee, payoff of credit balances or judgments on behalf of the veteran, funds for temporary buy downs (not discount points).
- The veteran is not allowed to pay for the wood destroying insect (termite) report; it is generally paid by the seller.

The VA is not a lender. VA loans are underwritten and approved directly by VA-approved lenders on behalf of the VA. The majority of loan transactions are handled directly by the lender with little VA intervention. However, the lender must be approved to issue VA loans.

Chapter 11
Before You Buy:
Evaluating Your Potential Home

Often, we hear from buyers that the buying process seemed like a whirlwind. One day they were looking at homes and the next thing they knew, they were under contract to purchase and scrambling to get organized. This is true of folks buying their first home and their tenth home.

If you are unprepared for the journey you are about to embark on – and buying a home is often the biggest financial event of your life – you will find yourself far too stressed to enjoy the fact that you are about to own a new home. But, buying a home does not have to be stressful. In fact, it is supposed to be fun.

The key to an enjoyable and stress-free purchase is really pretty simple: Be Prepared!

As we have discussed elsewhere, being prepared is essential to the home buying and financing process.

Before you even look at homes or apply for the mortgage, it is a good idea to understand the benefits of owning and define why you want to own a home or move to a new one. Hopefully, by now, you have already gone through this process and have decided that it is, in fact, a good idea to buy now. If not, now is a good time to make sure you are clear on the benefits for you and your family and dedicated to making the move.

Also be sure to clearly define your search parameters. First and foremost, get pre-approved for your financing. See the previous chapters for more on this. Getting pre-approved will save you untold amounts of stress, time and energy (and very possibly some hard-earned money).

Then, start the search. Most home searches today begin on the Internet. With just a few clicks of the mouse, home buyers can search through hundreds of online listings, view virtual tours, and sort through dozens of photographs and aerial shots of neighborhoods and homes. You've probably defined your goals and have a pretty good idea of the type of home and neighborhood you want. By the time you reach your real estate agent's office, you are halfway to home ownership.

While searching on line is great, do not underestimate the value of an experienced and reliable buyer's agent. Refer back to Chapter 5 for more information on Buyer's Agents.

Remember, we are in an historic buyer's market. You have choices – and you will certainly find several nice homes that fit your goals and your budget. Be sure to shop around and consider all aspects of your purchase. But then take action. Once you find a home that fits your needs, grab it!

Some tips for evaluation homes as you shop:

- Bring a digital camera and begin each series of photos with a close-up of the house number to identify where each group of home photos start and end.
- Take plenty of notes of unusual features, colors and design elements.
- Pay attention to the home's surroundings. What is next door? Do 2-story homes tower over your single story?
- If you have school-age children, check out the schools.

- Great Schools.Net is a GREAT resource for this.
- Do you like the location? Is it near a park or a power plant?
- Immediately after leaving, rate each home on a scale of 1 to 10, with 10 being the highest.

After you have had seen several good candidates, go back and look at your top three a second time. In fact, you will probably already know which one or two homes you would like to buy.

Also try to visit them at different times of day so you can get a feel for the neighborhood. Often, you will get a different feel for a home on a Saturday morning vs. a Wednesday afternoon. This can be a good or a bad thing – just be aware of it. And, don't be afraid to talk to the neighbors – after all, you may live near them for a long time to come.

At this point, you are ready to make your offer. If you are prepared, you will already have your financing in place and all you will need to do is call your mortgage professional. At the same time, your agent will call the listing agents to find out more about the sellers' motivation and to double-check that an offer hasn't come in, making sure these homes are still available to purchase. If all goes well, you will have a new home under contract. Congratulations. But your work is not done!

Before you are fully committed to the new purchase, be sure to get a reliable home inspector to do a thorough inspection (see Chapter 16 for more on home inspections). Ask your agent for a good referral and don't allow yourself to be pressured into ignoring defects that could come back to haunt you later. Now, with a contract and a positive home inspection, you are ready to sit back and relax a little while your lender and your agent handle all the details for you.

Chapter 12
Buying Foreclosed Homes and Short Sale Homes

Five Insider Tips

No one knows for sure when the housing downturn will finally hit bottom. But, one thing is for certain – housing prices are at rock-bottom levels and mortgage rates are at all-time lows. If you're looking to buy a home now - and plan to stay in it for a while - there are plenty of bargains to be had on a foreclosed property. Now is the time to buy. Don't worry about trying to time the absolute market bottom or you may miss out on a deal of a lifetime.

Banks are often willing to sell foreclosed homes for up to 20% or more below market value just to get these troubled properties off their books. With foreclosures at an all-time high in the past few years, there's no shortage of these opportunities to pursue. However, prospective buyers should know that closing on that super-cheap distressed home is often a lot more complicated and risky than buying a home that doesn't have all of that financial baggage.

Here are five things you should know before you buy a foreclosed home.

1. Finding Properties in Foreclosure

Thanks to the Internet, it's easier than ever to find homes in foreclosure. Between the internet and a good buyer's agent, you should have no problem finding plenty of options.

The biggest bargains can be found in areas where there's a large concentration of distressed properties. The banks with the most exposure to these areas are typically the most motivated to cut a deal since they don't want to get stuck with a ton of real estate they can't unload. But before you snap up the cheapest home you can find, make sure to do some research. Find out if the property is located in a decent neighborhood with good schools and healthy employment rates.

Remember, if you buy in an area that's losing jobs and is riddled with crime, home values are likely to take a lot longer to recover.

Homes can be bought with as little as $100 down; and usually no more than 5% down at most.

Don't shy away from homes that need some TLC. There are terrific loan options for those who wish to buy and fix up a home – with all of the costs of the renovation rolled into one loan at today's low rates. Renovations can be tiny or major, so virtually any kind of work can be included. And, there are even loans available to buy and renovate a home with as little as $100 down. See Chapter 10 for details.

2. Avoid Auctions

While there are a number of safe ways to buy a foreclosed property, bidding on one at a court auction isn't one of them. That's because you're buying a home sight unseen and without an inspection.

Also, auctions are designed to get the bidders excited and to bid more than they would normally offer. Plus, you'll have no idea whether the home needs repairs and how much they might cost. Some of these properties also owe back taxes, a headache that's transferred to the new owner.

And finally, in most cases, you'll need to pay cash for the home since you will need to settle the purchase within a very short time.

The least risky way to buy a foreclosed home is to wait until the bank has put it back onto the real estate market. These properties are called bank-owned or real estate-owned (REO). Before a bank hangs a "For Sale" sign, it pays off all the existing debts and taxes, and in many cases, repairs the home to bring it up to the standards of the neighborhood. Best of all, you should be able to buy a bank-owned property with a traditional mortgage.

3. Research Home Values

Just because a home is being sold by the bank, doesn't necessarily mean it's a bargain. Home prices have fallen dramatically from their peaks in 2006, a time when loose-lending practices allowed people of all credit ranks to easily obtain mortgages. Now, many homeowners going through the foreclosure process owe more on the mortgage than their property is actually worth. To make sure you aren't buying an overpriced home, research home values in the area. That way, you'll be better able to identify potential deals.

A Note Regarding Short Sales

If you fall in love with a home in pre-foreclosure that's overpriced, then you can see if the bank will allow a short sale. This is when the bank accepts less for the home than the amount owed on the mortgage. While not an ideal scenario, accepting a lower price is often in the bank's best interest. Banks typically spend $25,000 to $50,000 during the foreclosure process. On top of that, they typically end up reducing a home's asking price to match current market values, so they may be willing to negotiate now.

However, if you are pursuing a short sale, be prepared for a lengthy and stressful process. These deals take much longer than normal to secure – some negotiations go on for six months or more. Also, be sure to do your homework when choosing a short sale agent to work with – it seems everyone is jumping on the short sale band wagon, but very few actually know what they are doing.

4. Line Up Financing First

While it's always a good idea to get preapproved for a mortgage before you start shopping for a home, it's even more critical when you're shopping for foreclosed properties. Even if you have stellar credit, don't assume the financing will be as quick and easy as buying a non-foreclosure.

Also, some lenders will only offer a mortgage if the house is in decent condition. Fortunately, there are experts in dealing with these types of properties and they can help guide you through the process.

5. Get It Inspected

Even if a home is brand new you want to get it inspected. But inspections are especially important when you're dealing with homes in foreclosure. Often, when people have trouble paying their bills, they typically put off the regular maintenance on their homes.

Once a home is seized by a bank, it then sits vacant and falls even further into disrepair. In a worst-case scenario, a homeowner could be so angry he lost his home that he actively destroys a property before he moves out.

Without an inspection, you won't be able to estimate the cost for repairs or be able to report the home's true condition to your lender. For on home inspections, see Chapter 16.

Buying a foreclosure can be a great way to find the perfect home at a bargain price -- but, only if you are careful and follow these five insider tips. Don't let someone else's nightmare become yours.

Chapter 13
Buying Brand New - Tips on Buying From a Builder

Sometimes, it just has to be NEW. Whether it is a pair of new shoes, a new car, or a brand new home; sometimes it just has to be new. And for home buyers, there may be no better time to buy a new home from a builder than now. The recent downturn in the economy, along with the deepening housing slump, means builders are offering some great deals in order to sell their homes.

Buying new construction is much like buying an existing house. But, there are some things to watch for that you may not consider. Here are some Insider Tips on buying a new home from a builder. These tips apply to buying a home from the builder's existing inventory or buying before the home is completed.

Hire Your Own Agent

The builder's sales agents are paid to represent the builder, regardless of what they may tell you. Many will use high pressure tactics to persuade you to sign the contract. Due to the high volume nature of brand new home sales, lots of builder's agents are paid less than a traditional commission; some earn a salary plus incentives, so turnover is important to their livelihood.

Hire a Buyer's Agent to represent you. Most of the time, your agent will be paid by the seller, but sometimes the responsibility for the agent's fee is open for discussion. Even if you have to directly pay your agent, you can probably add that fee to the sales price, and it would be worth it because a good negotiating buyer's agent can save you thousands more than the commission.

Your own agent will represent you, and will be your fiduciary and is required to disclose the positives as well as the negatives about the transaction. Builder's agents don't discuss drawbacks.

If your contract contains a contingency to sell your existing home before buying, again, hire your own seller's agent to list your home. Be aware that buying before selling is not always in your best interest because hard bargaining goes out the window when you've emotionally moved out of your home. Additionally, with today's lending environment, it may be very difficult for most people to buy a new home before the old one is sold.

Get Pre-Approved for Your Mortgage

As we have discussed at length, be sure to get fully pre-approved before you shop for a new home.

Obtain Legal Advice Before Buying a Brand New Home

Particularly true with pre-construction - before you sign a purchase contract, talk to a real estate lawyer. Standard purchase agreements are designed to keep everybody out of court, but they don't necessarily contain language that protects the buyer.

Ask questions about removal of contingencies and your cancellation rights. Make sure you understand your liability and commitments.

Know How the House is Being Built

Find out if the materials used by the builder contain chemicals that are hazardous to your health. If your contract contains a warning about health issues, it's probably because it's a valid concern and other buyers have gone to court over it.

Verify Option and Upgrade Pricing

Determine which options and upgrades you want. Bear in mind that for many builders, the profit margin is highest in upgrades. Some builders can sell a home for almost bare construction cost because they make the bulk of their profit in the upgrades.

Also, be sure to discuss any options and upgrades with your lender. Most of the time, the costs of any options can be added into your loan. But, if the option costs exceed the value of the home, you may not be able to finance them and will have to pay for these in cash. Don't assume $10,000 worth of whatever upgrade will add $10,000 to your value. Builders are notorious for overcharging for options. Be sure the options are really worth the asking price.

Ask about cancellations and whether you will be held liable for items the builder cannot return to a vendor.

Some contracts give the builder the right to choose your upgrades if you do not submit your request within a certain period of time.

To save money, consider which upgrades you could purchase and install yourself after the purchase closes. However, realize that some upgrades such as CAT-V, DSS or security wiring inside the walls are easier to do before construction.

Check Out the Builder's Reputation

If a buyer has a bad experience with a builder, the word spreads rapidly throughout a community. But you won't know if a bad rep is an isolated experience or if the builder repeatedly brings bad publicity to itself without checking and verifying the public records for lawsuits.

Talk to the neighbors and scrutinize the construction quality of surrounding homes.

Find out whether the builder sells to investors. Some builders require all their homes to be owner occupied. Others eagerly sell as much inventory to investors as profit margins will allow. If the market suddenly dips, investors are typically the first to bail and, besides, part of the reason you are buying in a new subdivision is to be surrounded by other buyers just like you, not tenants.

Hire a Home Inspector

Always, always, always get a home inspection when you buy. And hire a licensed and accredited individual to perform the inspection -- not your dad or your buddy contractor, get a real inspector. Be there for the inspection and ask questions because a new home can contain defects. The HVAC system might be too small or the plumbing could be installed backwards. Construction workers make mistakes.

If the inspector calls for further inspection by another professional contractor, find out if the inspector is telling you there could be a serious issue or if the inspector isn't licensed to address that issue. For more on home inspections, see Chapter 16.

Chapter 14
Buying and Renovating a Fixer-Upper
(even with only $100 Down)

Renovation loans are great for folks who wish to buy and renovate a home. Perhaps you just cannot find the right house, but you can find an OK house in the right neighborhood. A renovation loan is the perfect solution.

Before these types of loans became available, homeowners had very few alternatives. They could basically pay for the improvements with cash, or do without.

Rehab and Renovation loans solve this problem. Now, loans can be made based on the future, renovated value of the property - all rolled into one loan at today's great rates.

There are several different loan programs for purchase and renovation, and almost all of them require minimal down payment and will roll all construction/renovation costs into the loan. You can even get a loan to buy and renovate a home with as little as $100 down.

Some good choices are the FHA 203K program (which can be combined with the FHA $100 Down program when buying from HUD inventory). Another is Fannie Mae's "Homepath" loan program. Remember, neither FHA nor Fannie Mae are actual lenders. You must find a lender that offers these programs.

Some Basic Facts About Renovation Loans

For all programs, you must be gainfully employed, able to document your income and have at least a 620 credit score, and 640 or 660 in many cases. If your scores are less than 620, please discuss your situation with your lender to explore your options. Most likely, you will need to first raise your scores before you can move forward with a loan.

Typically, loans in these programs have loan limits tied to the county of the property. They are usually fine for any home that does not require a "jumbo" loan.

Loans are intended for PRIMARY RESIDENCE ONLY.

Single Family Residences, Duplexes and 3-4 Unit Properties are acceptable. Different guidelines apply for 2-4 unit properties.

Loans will allow all rehab costs to be rolled into loan and will be approved based on the "after-renovated" value.

For Purchases: Sellers may contribute from 3%, and as much as 6% in some cases, towards your closing costs.

All work must be done using qualified contractors.

After purchase, you will have up to Six Months to complete renovations.

Minimum renovation amount is typically $5,000. Maximum is as much as you need, only subject to loan limits and your qualifications.

With these Purchase and Renovation Loans, you can:

- Borrow based on the "after-completed" value,

- Include all repairs in the mortgage,
- Eliminate health hazards (lead paint, for example),
- Make structural repairs and alterations (including additions),
- Remodel kitchens, bathrooms, etc.,
- Replace siding, roof, gutters, downspouts, etc.,
- Update plumbing, heating, electrical systems,
- Install or repair the well and/or septic systems,
- Replace flooring, carpeting or tile,
- Make energy conservation Improvements: Double pane windows and doors, insulation, caulking,
- Add decks, patios, fencing.

With these programs, you can also:

- Purchase and Renovate One to Four unit dwellings,
- Buy a Multi-unit dwellings and convert down to one to four units,
- Buy a Non-residential building and convert to residential,
- Buy a Single Family house and convert to a 2-4 units dwelling,
- Buy Mixed use properties (Commercial properties with residential units attached),
- Completely rebuild from the foundation (tear down and rebuild),
- Building MUST have had an Occupancy Certificate at one time (no brand new construction, this would require a construction loan).

Here is just a small list of the kinds of renovation work you can do to turn your house into your dream home:

- New freestanding appliances
- Bathroom remodels
- Master bedroom remodel
- Upgrading HVAC
- Adding energy efficient improvements
- Wells and septic repair and upgrades
- New siding
- Interior painting
- Exterior painting
- Attic build-outs
- Waterproofing the basement
- Creating a media room
- Adding a 2nd floor
- Total renovations
- Finishing the basement
- Bedroom additions
- Neck deck / patios
- New hardwood flooring
- New doors and windows
- Upgrading plumbing and electrical
- Opening up the floor plan
- New granite countertops
- Vaulting the ceilings
- Going GREEN!
- New fixtures for bathtubs, sinks and kitchens
- Making a house handicap accessible
- Getting a condo or house ready for a new college student
- Solar panels
- Low flow toilets and shower heads
- Creating a new master bedroom area
- Much, much more...

A renovation loan can be a great option in today's market. With all of the foreclosed and distressed homes on the market – many of which need some work – you may be able to find a great home at a great price and turn it into your dream home.

Chapter 15
8 Home Buyer Traps You MUST Avoid

Buying a home is probably going to be the largest financial investment you will ever make. It can be a daunting task. Throughout this book, you have learned several tips and insider secrets for making the process a smooth, stress-free, and enjoyable experience.

Now, here are eight tips that will help prevent you from:

- Paying too much for the home you want.
- Buying the wrong home for your needs.
- Losing out to another buyer for your dream home.

By remaining mindful of these traps, you will certainly end up with the right home at the right price with the right loan.

Trap #1: Not Working with the Right Professionals

Although this has been discussed elsewhere in this book, it is so important that it bears repeating. Buying a home is serious business and should not be treated like going out and buying an ice cream cone.

First time buyers, and even experienced buyers, need to surround themselves with a team that they can trust. Your team should include, at the very least: your mortgage professional, your buyer's agent, your title company and your home inspector. By assembling a team of competent and trustworthy professionals, you will help insure that your best interests are always met.

Trap #2: Failing to Research Your Purchase

Is the price being offered fair? Is it too high? Is it a great deal? If you fail to research the market – as it is today, not 3, 6 or 12 months ago – you will not understand what comparable homes are selling for in your neighborhood.

Making your offer without proper research is nothing more than playing the lottery. Sure, there is a chance you hit the jackpot. But there is a much better chance that you will part with more of your hard-earned money than is necessary.

It is easy to do this research. Start by working with a trustworthy buyer's agent. Ask them to give you a list of recently sold homes and their prices. Then, take the time to drive by the homes on that list to get a feel for the prices in the area and the types of homes and amenities that have been sold.

By doing so, you will quickly become educated as to the values of the homes in the area and be able to make an educated offer on your dream home.

Trap #3: Not Being Realistic

Before you ever start shopping for a home, it is important that you understand what you can and cannot afford. This is easily accomplished by finding a trustworthy loan professional and getting pre-approved.

There is no sense in shopping for homes you could never afford. Not only is this a waste of your time, it will only discourage you from finding the appropriate home for you and your family.

It is equally important to clearly know what you need and what you want in your new home. Knowing what you are really looking for in a home is perhaps a bit more complicated than it would seem.

It is it is important that you make a realistic "shopping list" in an attempt to narrow your choices of properties. Hunting for a home can be a time consuming process, especially if you have not determined in advance the parameters of your search.

Many home buyers make the mistake of misinterpreting a WANT as a NEED. As a result, they often dismiss homes that perfectly fit their needs in search for one that has their wants. This is not to say that you cannot have what you desire in your home--just that you must be able to differentiate between what you truly need and what you would like to have.

Your budget must be the determining factor here, not a "wish list." Note, also, that in the examples below, many WANTS can be changed in a particular home. If the house doesn't have all the features you want now, you can either change it later or use a Purchase and Renovation loan so you can have your "wants" now.

A few examples of NEEDS:

- Enough square footage for comfortable living
- Enough bedrooms to accommodate your family
- Adequate distance from work
- Adequate number of bathrooms
- Eat-in kitchen
- Garage or basement for storage needs

- Lot size to accommodate children's play area
- Adaptation for Handicapped
- Proximity to a specific school
- All living areas on single floor for health reasons

A few examples of WANTS:

- Carpeting color, paint color, exterior color, roof color, etc.
- Pool or Jacuzzi (unless for medical reasons)
- Wood floors
- Eat-in kitchen or Bay windows
- Built-in entertainment center
- Brass lighting fixtures
- Skylights
- A pretty view
- Specific brand/types of appliances

Take a few minutes to develop your own list of NEEDS and WANTS. Create a simple "Wants and Needs Scorecard and Recap Sheet" and stick to it as you shop.

You can use this tool as you begin to evaluate homes. The goal is to put the emphasis on finding a house that includes all of your needs and as many of your wants as is practical--yet remains in your budget. Once you have a clearer view of what your house will need to have, the next step, actually looking for a home, will be a great deal easier!

Trap #4: Unclear Title Issues

Make sure early in the buying process that there are not any title issues that would prevent you from owning your new home free and clear. If you are using a mortgage, your lender will do this for you. But if you are paying cash, you will want to make sure you initiate this yourself with your chosen title insurance company.

You will not be able to close on your loan if there are issues regarding the chain of title to the property. Most commonly, problems relate to liens on the property that were incurred by the previous owner. These can usually be quickly resolved. However, there are times when there are bigger issues that may seriously delay, or even prevent, your purchase.

Trap #5: Inaccurate or Misleading Surveys

As part of your offer to purchase, make sure you request – no demand – an updated property survey. A survey is simply a marking of your property boundaries. You will receive a drawing, done precisely, that shows the outline of your property.

If the survey is not current, you may find that there have been changes that are not shown, such as additions to the house, a new pool, or a neighbor's fence that is across your property line.

You may also discover that the property is not actually what has been represented.

I'll share a short, very true, story of what happened to a client who ignored my advice a few years ago. Please note that while most loan programs require a current survey, not all do. So it is your responsibility to make sure you know what you are buying.

123

My client, I won't tell you his name to protect the dumb, searched and searched for a piece of land to build his dream house. He was in an area where there just wasn't much land available at any price, let alone a lot he could afford. After nearly a year and a half of looking, he called me one day to tell me he had finally found the perfect 3 acre lot at the right price of $180,000.

He immediately offered a $10,000 non-refundable deposit (as he was already pre-approved, he thought he was safe in doing this – NEVER make a deposit that is non-refundable until every condition of the contract is met. Working with a good buyer's agent will help you not make this mistake). The construction to permanent loan program did not require a new survey. We suggested that he get one, but he choose to save the $200 it would have cost.

During the contract period for the construction loan, my client had to get his home plans and his various construction bids. This took both time and money. It took about 60 days and cost around $5,000.

The loan process went smoothly and the day of closing arrived. The closing itself went off without a hitch. The closing happened on a Friday afternoon. The next morning, Saturday, he went out to his new property, plans in hand, to walk around and imagine where everything would go. As he was sticking a small stake in the ground to mark one of the corners of his new dream home, his neighbor stopped by and asked…

"What are you doing on my property?"

Well, my client explained that he has just bought the land and was planning to build his new home here. The friendly

124

neighbor then explained that the spot they were standing on was *his* land, and had certainly not been sold.

To make a long story, short, the 3 acres that my client "thought" he was buying turned out to be 1.42 acres – less than half of what he was sold!! The property was not even big enough to hold the boundaries of the house he was planning on building.

After a 15month legal battle, over $20,000 in legal fees and the loss of the money he had spent on the plans and the loan closing (all told, over $30,000 lost), my client was able to "settle" his battle and get out of the deal.

Saving $200 on a survey cost him over $30,000 and the chance to build his dream home.

Trap # 6: Undisclosed Deferred Maintenance or Problems

You should not expect every seller you meet to tell you the truth about his property. Heck, if you knew the roof had been leaking for the last 3 years, you may not want to buy the house.

While most people are basically honest, you may find yourself buying from someone who is trying to deceive you about the condition of their home. Especially in a buyer's market, where is may be tough to sell a home, you need to be aware of this issue and protect yourself.

The solution is simple: hire a qualified Home Inspector. We spend an entire chapter of this book trying to convince you to do so; that is how important it is.

Yes, you will pay the cost of this inspection – anywhere from $300 to $500 in most areas. You can even include that cost in your closing costs, if those costs are being paid for by the seller. But, even if they are not, it is a tiny price to pay for the peace of mind that comes with knowing that the biggest investment you may ever make is a sound one.

Trap #7: Not Getting Your Mortgage Pre-Approval

I know this has also been discussed throughout this book, but it is very important to understand that a pre-approval is fast, easy and free. When you have your loan fully pre-approved, you will be able to shop for your new home with the confidence that you are actually able to buy it when you find the right one.

You will also be able to negotiate with the seller from a position of strength when the seller knows you are pre-approved and able to close on time.

What is a full pre-approval?

A full pre-approval requires that you provide all of the requested documents to your mortgage professional. Your lender will run a credit report and also verify things like your income and assets. Your file will go before an underwriter and will be stamped as approved, pending a clean appraisal and title report. As long as the few remaining conditions are met – and your situation does not change in the interim, your loan will close without problems.

Trap #8: Failing to Meet Contract Obligations

If your seller fails to comply with your sales contract by neglecting to address any repair items or issues you have negotiated, your closing could be delayed or even cancelled.

Your buyer's agent should help you negotiate, in the contract, an agreed upon amount of money to be placed in escrow if the seller fails to follow through on his obligations. Some loan programs will not even allow you to close until certain problems are fixed.

Then, be sure to do a full and complete walk through prior to closing. You may even need to call back your home inspector to assist you with this if the repairs were major items.

These are eight seemingly obvious traps that you need avoid. Unfortunately, far too many buyers (both first time and seasoned buyers) ignore the obvious. Don't allow yourself to fall into this trap.

Chapter 16
Home Inspections:
Why You Want (and Need) One.

You may have thought that finding the home of your dreams was a tough job, but you must make sure that the dream does not quickly become a nightmare.

Once you find the perfect home in the perfect neighborhood, don't assume all is well until you have a professional home inspector give you their seal of approval. Remember, if the home you are about to purchase does not have the structural integrity to give you peace of mind, you may be buying into a money pit and sleepless nights.

A home consists of many complex components including structural framing, physical components, electrical, plumbing, heating, and air-conditioning systems. It is important to know what is under the cosmetics. Sure, the bathrooms and kitchen look nice. Perhaps the wallpaper is not your taste but you figure you can take it down, along with that 1970's paneling in the playroom. But what is happening beneath the surface? Are there any surprises lurking? This is exactly the reason you need a competent home inspection engineer to assist you with the evaluation of the home's major systems.

Hiring a Professional

Be sure to retain a home inspection company with top

credentials. A Licensed Professional Engineer is a good credential to look for. If you want your home inspection conducted by a Licensed Professional Engineer (P.E.), be sure that your home inspection report will be stamped with the home inspector's licensed P.E. seal. The practice of engineering is State regulated and licensed; the P.E. seal on the home inspection report is the key to your protection.

Consumers who retain the services of a home inspector who is not a P.E., may be faced with paying a second home inspection fee if the home inspector uncovers a problem, such as a structural defect, that requires the opinion of a Licensed Professional Engineer. It makes the most sense to retain the services of an inspection company that is licensed to practice engineering right from the start.

A lot of information will be provided to you at the time of inspection; it's difficult to absorb it all. Terminology like heat exchanger, over fused circuit, plumbing vent stack, steel flitch plate, etc. may not sound like oven, sink, and entrance stairway, but these are terms that are part of a home. That is why you should be sure that your home inspection report will be a detailed written report, not a hand written checklist that is given to you at the conclusion of the home inspection. A checklist may not provide all of the information and engineering advice you need.

Home inspectors come in various shapes and sizes with a multitude of backgrounds. Be sure that the home inspection company you retain has professional affiliations, such as NABIE (National Academy Of Building Inspection Engineers) and NSPE (National Society Of Professional Engineers). Unlike home inspection trade societies (and there are many), NABIE and NSPE accept only Licensed Professional

Engineers as members. Members of NABIE need to meet tough entrance requirements, are highly qualified in the home inspection profession, and adhere to a strict code of ethics.

Don't be confused by home inspector "certifications" offered by, or sold by trade societies or companies, or obtained via home inspection home study courses. These certifications are available to anybody; a high school diploma is not even a requirement.

Things to Know Before the Inspection

After you have found and hired a good home inspector, be sure to attend the home inspection. One picture is worth a thousand words; make every effort to attend your home inspection.

Be sure that the home inspector is well equipped. The home inspection engineer should be fully equipped with necessary engineering tools including electrical testers, a fuel gas and carbon monoxide detector, moisture meter, ladder, inspection mirror, flashlight, level, and other home inspection tools, etc.

Be sure to follow the home inspector and ask questions. Do not be afraid to ask lots of questions - this is what you are paying for. This is perhaps the biggest investment of your life, so be proactive and make sure you fully understand everything that is happening.

Be sure that all of the following points are fully covered:

- The physical, plumbing, heating, air-conditioning, and electrical systems should be thoroughly inspected and evaluated.

- The home inspection engineer should determine the condition of the roof surface, the exterior facades, doors and windows.

- The land grading around the home should be examined, as well as the condition of decks, patios, porches, driveways and sidewalks.

- The physical condition of the interior of the home should be evaluated searching for telltale signs of problems.

- The engineer should determine if there are indications of past water intrusion into the attic or lower levels of the home and whether the home is susceptible to water intrusion in these areas.

- The home inspection engineer should look for materials that may be asbestos containing materials. The home inspection should include an inspection for wood destroying insects that will be accepted by your mortgage lender. If it is not included here, a separate Termite Inspection will be required.

- The home inspection engineer should inspect all electrical and mechanical components of the home and look for aluminum electrical distribution wires, electrical systems that are not adequate for modern usage, lead and galvanized steel water supply pipes, aged and inefficient heating and air-conditioning systems, etc.

- If the home has a well and/or septic system, these systems should be evaluated as well by the home inspector.

- Where applicable, consider optional testing of underground storage tanks, testing paint for lead, testing drinking water for lead, testing well supplied drinking water for bacteria, testing for radon gas in air, testing for urea formaldehyde foam insulation, etc.

After the inspection is complete, be sure to have the home inspection engineer summarize the findings and obtain a full verbal report at the conclusion of the inspection. The home inspection engineering report should be available the next working day after the home inspection.

At the conclusion of the inspection you should know the condition of the home you are purchasing, including all positive and negative aspects. You should know what repairs are needed, as well as the urgency of the needed repairs, and the magnitude of the repair costs. You should know a proper course of corrective repairs and whether alternatives are available. You should know if there are any unsafe conditions, and whether there are any risks of hidden deterioration.

You should expect an easy to understand detailed written home inspection report (not just a checklist). Also look for the Licensed Professional Engineer's P.E. seal at the end of the home inspector's report.

You should also expect the home inspection engineer to provide the answers to any questions you may have regarding the report. You should expect the engineer's door to be open for answers to future questions.

You should not expect the home inspector to offer to repair, for a fee, any uncovered defects (that would be a conflict of interest and may erode confidence you may have in the home inspector's findings).

If the report shows some problems you were not aware of, you will have to make some decisions about how to proceed. You should discuss these issues with your buyer's agent and determine if you will pay for these things, have the seller pay for them, or negotiate some middle ground.

Remember, there's rarely a perfect home. A good engineer will always find some defects but you need to weigh the positives against the negatives.

7 Insider Tips
Defects Every Home Inspection Should Look For

1) Exterior

Wear on a roof may be readily apparent if the wear is very advanced but a roof that is starting to age is a more subtle defect that the engineer can uncover. Resurfacing a roof costs thousands of dollars, and will cost much more if the existing roofing surface needs to be removed prior to re-roofing. If a roof will need to be resurfaced in the foreseeable future, this may be a negotiable item. Similarly, the siding of the house should be carefully inspected because residing a house can also cost thousands of dollars. Replacement of old defective windows can cost thousands of dollars, don't overlook this obvious defect. Eliminating problems before they start is smart, for example, the engineer should be sure that the land around the home is properly graded to divert water away from the home; this will help to reduce the possibility of water intrusion into the home.

2) Interior

If there's one defect you don't want to find out about after you move in, it's a basement that floods. The basement areas of the home should be thoroughly checked for signs of water intrusion, such as water stains, mildew, odor of dampness, efflorescence on the walls and floors, damaged and cupping floors. In addition, look for water proofing systems, sump pumps, etc. in the basement; these systems can help to reduce the risk of water flooding into the basement but may not be able to eliminate water intrusion under all conditions. If a house needs water proofing measures, the cost can run into the thousands.

Proper insulation and ventilation in a home should not be overlooked; proper ventilation in a home is more important than most home buyers are aware of. Inadequate ventilation in an attic results in accelerated deterioration of the structural roof deck; if this occurs, a major expense will be incurred to remove and replace the roofing shingles and roof deck, and in extreme cases, the roof rafters. This is one defect that should not be overlooked.

The condition of the paint surface on homes constructed prior to 1978 may contain lead paint which can be a problem if there is wide spread deterioration of the paint surface; your home inspection engineer may suggest an X-ray evaluation of the paint surface for lead content. If you are planning renovation of walls, etc. after you move in, lead paint is an issue to consider.

3) Structural

Bulges, deflections, and other irregularities in the roof, exterior wall framing, and interior framing, or cracks in the foundation wall may indicate a serious structural problem that may be the result of poor structural design, poor construction techniques, improper structural alteration, water damage, or termite damage. Jacking up a house to replace damaged structural components, or underpinning a defective foundation wall is a major expense.

The home inspection engineer has the experience, education and expertise to evaluate structural problems; this is one of the reasons why retaining the services of a Licensed Professional Engineer (P.E.) to conduct your home inspection instead of a home inspector who is not licensed to practice engineering is advantageous. Sure, anybody can report that a structural defect exists, but only a P.E. is licensed to offer a professional engineering judgment and design to correct the problem. Home buyers who do not retain the services of a P.E. may have to pay a second fee to obtain a professional engineer's opinion.

4) Electrical System

First, the engineer should determine the size of the service to determine if it meets current standards; bringing an upgraded electrical service into a home can cost one thousand dollars. The electrical system should then be checked by removing the cover from the electric service panel. Once the wiring is exposed, be sure that the home inspection engineer looks for problems in the panel such as burned wiring, overloaded circuits (the fuse or circuit breaker is too large for the wire size), improper wiring connections, openings in the panel (where a child can put their finger in the panel, ouch!), home owner installed wiring, etc.

In addition, electrical switches and convenience outlets in the house should be checked for open ground and wiring reversal conditions. Throughout the house, dead ended wiring and exposed wiring should be on the list of defects to look for. Homes wired in the mid 60's to mid-70's may have aluminum wiring and if so, the engineer should determine if an approved retrofit has been installed at the wiring connections; if not, a potential fire safety hazard exists. If the home is very old, it may have "knob and tube" wiring. This is ancient wiring and may be hazardous. Extensive wiring replacement can cost thousands of dollars.

5) Plumbing System

First, the home inspection engineer should determine the type of pipe that supplies water to the house from the municipal main in the street. Be wary of old lead and galvanized steel water supply pipes, replacement costs thousands of dollars. Be sure that your home inspection engineer checks the piping distribution in the house for type of material and condition looking for deterioration, incompatible piping materials, and leaks.

Your engineer should carry a moisture meter to evaluate any suspect plaster or wall board on the ceilings and walls caused by water leaks; replacing the piping network in the walls and ceilings is a major expense that can cost thousands of dollars. Be sure that the engineer checks all of the fixtures and faucets for proper operation, and also checks tiled bathtub and shower enclosures for integrity. Replacement of tiling in a bathroom, or replacement of a shower pan can cost a couple of thousand dollars.

6) Heating and Air Conditioning Systems

Look out for that old clunker that used to fire coal; it will consume fuel faster than you can feed it; plan on replacing it with a modern efficient heating system. Other problems include defective furnace heat exchangers, this type of problem is not always easy to uncover and usually means that the furnace will require replacement and this can cost three to four thousand dollars.

Boilers that are starting to leak will also require replacement and a typical cost is three to five thousand dollars; your engineer should look for these major defects.

In addition, your engineer should be sure that the heat distribution is satisfactory and that the heat distribution piping or ductwork is in good condition. Safety concerns such as defective controls, inoperative emergency switches, and evidence of past malfunctions and carbon monoxide emissions must be carefully investigated by the engineer.

Also be careful of special problems associated with radiant floor heating and other less common systems.

The engineer should advise you to have underground oil storage tanks tested for integrity; a leaking underground oil storage tank can cause thousands of dollars of environmental damage. Another environmental concern is the existence of insulation that may contain asbestos and is especially hazardous if the material is friable. The engineer should advise you to have any suspect material laboratory tested.

The home inspection engineer should test the central air-conditioning system to be sure that it is cooling properly; replacement of an air-conditioning compressor can cost two to five thousand dollars.

7) Deferred Maintenance

Be very careful of homes where deferred maintenance is clearly evident; if a home has been poorly maintained and there are obvious problems, proceed with extreme caution, this could be your worst nightmare. If there are obvious problems, imagine what you can't see; it's your money pit, keep your checkbook handy.

Remember, there are great deals on "handyman's specials," as long as you secure the proper financing to cover all of the costs of the repairs so that your new house becomes an up to date and safe dream home.

Be careful of homes where there is obvious plumbing and electrical work, as well as structural additions and renovations that were not professionally installed and were most likely installed by the home owner. Correcting these defects can cost thousands of dollars. This is a situation where the seller of the home is a weekend warrior who is well intentioned but has no clue regarding proper construction and trade practices; don't end up writing checks for work that the seller did not want to pay for.

Remember, to retain the services of a home inspector who issues a full written report detailing what is wrong, why it's wrong, and what needs to be done to correct the uncovered defects. Home inspection reports that consist of check lists handed to you at the end of an inspection are often missing necessary detail. Simply checking off good, fair poor, adequate, inadequate, etc. often leaves you wondering what to do next. Be sure that you retain services of an engineer whose door is open for future questions. This is not a time to be cheap. Hiring the right, qualified home inspector can save you thousands of dollars and untold stress.

Chapter 17
Real Estate and Mortgage Terms
It Pays to Know the Lingo

As we near the conclusion of this book, I thought it would be helpful to share some of the terminology of the real estate and mortgage industry. Those of us who do this every day take it for granted that we understand what is being said. I even catch myself at times using terms or phrases with a client, only to realize he or she has no idea what I am saying.

As a first time home buyer, there is certainly no shame in not understanding a term that your mortgage professional or Realtor uses. Just be sure to ask for clarification so that you do not miss an important point along the way.

Here is a list of common mortgage lending terminology. Use this list to refer back to whenever you need.

Adjustable Rate Mortgage (ARM): Mortgage loans under which the interest rate is periodically adjusted to more closely coincide are agreed to at the inception of the loan.

Alternative Documentation: The use of pay stubs, W-2 forms, and bank statements in lieu of Verifications of Employment (VOE) and Verifications of Deposit (VOD) to qualify a borrower for a mortgage.

Amortization: The systematic and continuous payment of an obligation through installments until the debt has been paid in full.

Annual Percentage Rate (APR): A term used in the Truth-in-Lending Act to present the percentage relationship of the total finance charge to the amount of the loan. The APR reflects the cost of the mortgage loan as a yearly rate. It could be higher than the interest rate stated on the Note because it includes, in addition to the interest rate, loan discount points, miscellaneous fees and mortgage insurance.

Appraisal: A report made by a qualified person setting forth an opinion or estimate of property value. (Appraisal also refers to the process through which a conclusion on property value is derived.)

Appraisal Amount or Appraised Value: The fair market value of a home determined by an independent appraisal. The appraisal uses local real estate market sales activity as a major basis for valuation.

Appreciation: An increase in the value of a property due to market conditions or other causes. The opposite is depreciation.

Balloon Mortgage: A fixed-rate mortgage for a set number of years and then must be paid off in full in a single "balloon" payment. Balloon loans are popular with borrowers expecting to sell or refinance their property within a definite period of time.

Bankruptcy: Legal relief from the payment of all debts after the surrender of all assets to a court-appointed trustee. Assets are distributed to creditors as full satisfaction of debts, with certain priorities and exemptions. A person, firm or corporation may declare bankruptcy under one of several chapters of the U. S. Bankruptcy Code: Chapter 7 covers liquidation of the debtor's assets; Chapter 11 covers reorganization of bankrupt businesses; Chapter 13 covers payment of debts by individuals through a bankruptcy plan.

Broker: Essentially, a mortgage "middle man." While there are some good brokers out there, you must remember that brokers are not direct lenders, they basically compile offers from various lenders and then re-sell them to the borrower. Brokers do not work for the lender and they have no direct interaction with the decision makers during the loan underwriting process. Although it is typically better to deal with a direct lender, brokers can sometimes find lower rates and better prices than the direct lender due to their ability to shop the loan to various lenders.

Cap: The limit placed on adjustments that can be made to the interest rate or payments such as the annual cap on an adjustable rate loan (ARM) or the cap on a rate over the life of the loan.

Cash-out Refinance: To refinance the mortgage on a property for more than the principal owed. This allows the borrower to get cash from the equity in their home. Loan products may vary on how much can be borrowed on a cash-out refinance.

Client Coordinator (CC): Some agents and loan officers use a Client Coordinator. The Client Coordinator sets the tone throughout the application process and ensures that each customer is kept informed of all needs and status through clear and concise communication.

Closer: The person who coordinates the closing time with the Client Coordinator and reviews and prepares the necessary closing documents.

Closing: Also known as settlement (or in some areas as "closing escrow"). This is the finalization of the process of purchasing or refinancing real estate. The closing includes the delivery of a Deed, the signing of Notes and the disbursement of funds

Closing Costs: Costs that are due at closing, in addition to the purchase price of the property. These costs normally include, but are not limited to, origination fee, discount points, attorney's fees, costs for title insurance, surveys, recording documents, and prepayment of real estate taxes and insurance premiums held by the lender. Sometimes the seller will help the borrower pay some of these costs.

Closing Statement: An accounting of the debits and credits incurred at closing. All FHA, VA and Conventional financing loans use a Uniform Closing or Settlement Statement commonly referred to as the "HUD-1."

Co-Borrower: A party who signs the mortgage note along with the primary borrower, and who also shares title to the subject real estate.

Collateral: Property pledged as security for a debt. For example, real estate that secures a mortgage. Collateral can be repossessed if the loan is not repaid.

Combined Loan To Value (CLTV): The mathematical relationship between the total of all loan amounts (first mortgage plus subordinate liens) and the value of the subject property.

Community Reinvestment Act (CRA): This act requires financial institutions to meet the credit needs of their community, including low and moderate-income sections of the local community. It also requires banks to make reports concerning their investment in the areas where they do business.

Condominium: A form of property ownership in which the homeowner holds title to an individual dwelling unit, an undivided interest in common areas of a multi-unit project, and sometimes the exclusive use of certain limited common areas. All condominiums must meet certain investor requirements.

Conforming Loan: A loan with a mortgage amount that does not exceed that which is eligible for purchase by FNMA or FHLMC. All loans are considered as conforming or non-conforming, also known as jumbo. In 2011, the conforming limit is $417,000.

Conventional Loan: A mortgage loan not insured or guaranteed by the federal government. FHA and VA loans are two examples of loans that are insured by the federal government.

Conversion Option: Options to convert an adjustable rate mortgage or balloon loan to a fixed rate mortgage under specified conditions.

Co-Signer: A party who signs the mortgage note along with the borrower, but who does not own or have any interest in the title to the property.

Creditor: A person to whom debt is owed by another person who is the "debtor".

Credit Rating: A rating given a person or company to establish credit-worthiness based upon present financial condition, experience and past credit history.

Credit Report: A document completed by a credit-reporting agency providing information about the buyer's credit cards, previous mortgage history, bank loans and public records dealing with financial matters.

Deal Structure: An Underwriters review of certain aspects of a loan application that do not meet standard guidelines.

Debt to Income Ratio: Compares the amount of monthly income to the amount the borrower will owe each month in house payment (PITI) plus other debts. The other debts may include but not limited to car payment, credit cards, alimony, child support, and personal loans. This ratio is commonly used to see if the borrower has the capacity to repay the debt. Typically, there will be a "front" ratio and a "back" ratio. The front ratio is simply your monthly PITI divided by your gross monthly income. The back ratio is your PITI + all other debts divided by your gross monthly income.

Deed of Trust: A legal document that conveys title to real estate to a disinterested third party (trustee) who holds the title until the owner of the property has repaid the debt. In states where it is used, a Deed of Trust accomplishes essentially the same purpose as a Mortgage.

Default: Failure to comply with the terms of any agreement. In real estate, generally used in connection with a mortgage obligation to refer to the failure to comply with the terms of the Promissory Note. Most often this default is a failure to make payments, however, there are other means by which a borrower may default, such as the failure to pay real estate taxes.

Depreciation: A decline in the value of property. The opposite of appreciation.

Discount Points: A percentage of the loan amount which is charged or credited by the lender upon making a mortgage loan. Loans that are made at the present market rate, with no points, are considered to be made at "par." Because of the lender's ability to charge or credit points on an individual loan,

146

the lender is able to tailor a loan program and interest rate to fit the needs of each individual borrower. Discount points can be negotiated in the Purchase Contract to be paid by either the seller or the borrower.

Each point equals 1% of the mortgage loan. For example, a charge of 1 point on a $50,000 loan would result in a charge of $500; ½ point would be $250 ($50,000 x .50%).

Down Payment: The part of the purchase price which the buyer pays in cash and does not finance with a mortgage.

Earnest Money: Deposit made by a purchaser of real estate as evidence of good faith.

Equal Credit Opportunity Act (ECOA): Also known as Regulation B. A federal law that prohibits a lender from discriminating in mortgage lending on the basis of race, color, religion, national origin, sex, marital status, age, income derived from public assistance programs, or previous exercise of Consumer Credit Protection Act rights.

Equity: The difference between the current market value of a property and the principal balance of all outstanding loans.

Escrow Account: An account held by the lending institution to which the borrower pays monthly installments for property taxes, insurance, and special assessments, and from which the lender disburses these sums as they become due.

Fair Credit Reporting Act: Regulated the collection and distribution of information by the consumer credit reporting industry. It also affects how financial institutions collect and convey credit information about loan applicants or borrowers.

Fair Housing Act: Prohibits the denial or variance of the terms of real estate related transactions based on race, color, religion, sex, national origin, disability, or familiar status of the credit applicant. Real estate related transactions include a mortgage, home improvement, or other loans secured by a dwelling.

Federal Home Loan Mortgage Corporation (FHLMC): Also known as Freddie Mac. A publicly owned corporation created by Congress to support the secondary mortgage market. It purchases and sells conventional residential mortgages as well as residential mortgages insured by the Federal Housing Administration (FHA) or guaranteed by the Veterans Administration (VA).

Federal National Mortgage Association (FNMA): Also known as Fannie Mae. A privately owned corporation to support the secondary mortgage market. It adds liquidity to the mortgage market by investing in home loans through the country.

FICO Score: A credit score given to a person that establishes creditworthiness based on present financial condition, experience and past credit history.

Finance Charge: The cost of credit as a dollar amount (i.e. total amount of interest and specific other loan charges to be paid over the term of the loan and other loan charges to be paid by the borrower at closing). Loan charges include origination fees, discount points, mortgage insurance, and other applicable charges. If the seller pays any of these charges, they cannot be included in the finance charge.

Financial Statement: A summary of facts showing an individual's or company's financial condition. For individuals, it states their assets and liabilities as of a given date. For a company it should include a Profit and Loss Statement (P&L)

for a certain period of time and balance sheet, stating assets and liabilities as of a given date.

First Mortgage: A real estate loan that creates a primary lien against real property.

First Rate Adjustment – First rate adjustment after: In association with an Adjustable Rate Mortgage loan, this is the number of months after which the loan has closed when the first interest rate adjustment will occur.

First Rate Adjustment – Maximum rate decrease: In association with an Adjustable Rate Mortgage loan, this is the most the interest rate can decrease during the first adjustment period.

First Rate Adjustment – Maximum rate increase: In association with an Adjustable Rate Mortgage loan, this is the most the interest rate can increase during the first adjustment period.

Fixed Rate Mortgage: The type of loan where the interest rate will not change for the entire term of the loan.

Floating: The term used when a purchaser elects not to lock-in an interest rate at the time of application.

Flood Insurance: Insurance that compensates for direct physical damages by or from flood to the insured property subject to the terms, provisions; conditions and losses not covered provision of the policy. It is required for mortgages on properties located in federally designated flood areas. Every mortgage will require a "flood cert" that tells the lender whether or not your property is in a flood zone.

Good Faith Estimate (GFE): An estimate of settlement charges paid by the borrower at closing. The Real Estate Settlement

Procedures Act (RESPA) requires a Good Faith Estimate of settlement charges be provided to the borrower.

Gift Letter: A letter or affidavit that indicates that part of a borrower's down payment is supplied by relatives or friends in the form of a gift and that the gift does not have to be repaid.

Gross Income: A person's income before deduction for income taxation.

Hazard Insurance: Insurance against losses caused by perils which are commonly covered in policies described as a "Homeowner Policy".

Home Maintenance: Costs associated with maintaining a home. This may include, but not limited to, general repairs, replacement or repair of furnace, air conditioning, roof, plumbing and electrical systems.

Home Mortgage Disclosure Act (HMDA): Also known as Regulation C. The purpose of HMDA is to provide disclosure of mortgage lending application activity (home purchase or improvement) to regulators and the public. Information is collected on each application, and is recorded on a log that is compiled to produce a report on application activity by geographic designation (census tract).

Homeowners Association (HOA): A non-profit corporation or association that manages common areas and services of a Condominium or Planned Unit Development (PUD).

Homeowners Insurance: Insurance that covers damage to the insured's residence and liability claims made against the insured subject to the policy terms, conditions, provisions, losses not insured provision and exclusions.

Housing Expense Ratio: Ratio used to determine the borrowers capacity to repay a home loan. The ratio compares monthly income to the house payment (Principal, Interest, Taxes and Insurance).

HUD1: see Closing Statement

Income to Debt Ratio: See Debt to Income Ratio.

Index: In connection with ARM loans, the external measurement used by a Lender to determine future changes which are to occur to an adjustable loan program. These will typically be published rates that are independent of the Lender's control, such as a Treasury Bill. To calculate your ARM rate, you would add the index rate + the loan's "margin." (see also Margin).

Initial Interest Rate: The beginning interest rate at the start of an adjustable rate mortgage (ARM). It may be lower than the fully indexed rate or "going market rate" and it will remain constant until it is adjusted up or down on the adjustment date.

Interest: The amount paid by a borrower to a lender for the use of the lender's money for a certain period of time. The amount paid by a bank on some deposit accounts.

Interest Income: The potential income from funds which would have been used for the down payment, closing costs, and any difference (increase) between monthly rental payment and monthly mortgage payment.

Interest Rate: The percentage of an amount of money that is paid for its use for a specific time; usually expressed as an annual percentage.

Judgment: Decree of a court declaring that one individual is indebted to another and fixing the amount of such indebtedness.

Jumbo Loan: A loan above the limit set by the Federal National Mortgage Association (Fannie Mae) and the Federal Home Loan Mortgage Corporation (Freddie Mac). Also referred to as a non-conforming loan.

Late Charge: An additional charge a borrower is required to pay as a penalty for failure to pay a regular mortgage loan installment when due; a penalty for a delinquent payment.

Lien: A legal claim against a property that must be paid off when the property is sold. A lien is created when you borrow money and use your home as collateral for the loan.

Life of Loan – Maximum rate decrease: In association with an Adjustable Rate Mortgage loan, this is the most the interest can decrease over the life of the mortgage loan.

Life of Loan – Maximum rate increase: In association with an Adjustable Rate Mortgage loan, this is the most the interest can increase over the life of the mortgage loan.

Loan Application: A source of information on which the lender bases a decision to make or not make a loan; defines the terms of the loan contract, gives the names of the borrower(s), place of employment, salary, bank accounts, credit references, real estate owned, and describes the property to be mortgaged. Typically the loan application is taken on form 1003. See Chapter 6 for more details on the form 1003.

Loan Balance: The amount of remaining unpaid principal balance owed by the borrower.

Loan Term: Number of years a loan is amortized. Mortgage loan terms are generally 15, 20, or 30 years.

Loan-to-Value (LTV): The ratio of the total amount borrowed on a mortgage against a property, compared to the appraised value of the property. A LTV ratio of 90 means that the borrower is borrowing 90% of the value of the property and paying 10% as a down payment. For purchases, the value of the property is the lesser of the purchase price or the appraised value. For refinances the value is determined by an appraisal.

Loan-to-Value Ratio: The ratio, expressed as a percentage, of the amount of the loan (numerator) to the value or selling price of real property (denominator). For example, if you have an $80,000 1st mortgage on a home with an appraised value of $100,000, the LTV is 80% ($80,000 / $100,000 = 80%).

Lock-In: A written agreement between the lender and borrower for a specified period of time in which the lender will hold a specific interest rate, origination and/or discount point(s).

Margin: Under the terms of an adjustable rate mortgage (ARM), the margin is a set adjustment to the index. The particular loan product determines the amount of the margin.

Median Income: The middle income level. Half of the incomes would be higher than the median income and half of the incomes would be below the median income. This is not to be confused with an average income.

Mortgage: The written instrument used to pledge a title to real estate as security for repayment of a Promissory Note.

Mortgage Insurance: Insurance written in connection with a mortgage loan that indemnifies the lender in the event of borrower default. In connection with conventional loan transactions, this insurance is commonly referred to as Private Mortgage Insurance (PMI). With government insured loans, it is referred to as MIP. Any government-insured loan or any conventional loan with an LTV above 80% will require insurance.

Mortgage Note: A written promise to pay a sum of money at a stated interest rate during a specified term. It is typically secured by a mortgage.

Mortgage Servicing: Controlling the necessary duties of a mortgagee, such as collecting payments, releasing the lien upon payment in full, foreclosing if in default, and making sure the taxes are paid, insurance is in force, etc. The lender or a company acting for the lender, for a servicing fee, may do servicing. (Also called Loan Servicing.)

Mortgagee: The institution, group, or individual that lends money on the security of pledged real estate; the association, the lender.

Mortgagee Clause: This is the clause that is typically used for hazard insurance and flood insurance. For loans originated by the Example Bank it may read: Example Bank, F.S.B., Its Successor and/or Assigns, P.O. Box 1234, Anytown, NJ 12345-6789.

Mortgagor: The owner of real estate who pledges his property as security for the repayment of a debt; the borrower.

Net Income: The difference between effective gross income and expense including taxes and insurance. The term is qualified as net income before depreciation and debt.

Non-Conforming: A loan with a mortgage amount that exceeds that which is eligible for purchase by FNMA or FHLMC. All other loans above this amount are considered to be non-conforming or jumbo loans.

Non-Owner-Occupied Property: Property purchased by a borrower not for a primary residence but as an investment with the intent of generating rental income, tax benefits, and profitable resale.

Note: A written promise by one party to pay a specific sum of money to a second party under conditions agreed upon mutually. Also called "promissory note."

Note Rate: The interest rate on the mortgage loan.

Origination Fee: A fee paid to a lender for processing a loan application; it is stated as a percentage of the mortgage amount.

Origination Process: Process in which a lender solicits business, gathers required information and commits to loan money, for the purchase of real estate.

Owner-Occupied Property: The borrower or a member of the immediate family lives in the property as a primary residence.

PITI: Term commonly used to refer to a mortgage loan payment. Acronym stands for Principal, Interest, Taxes, and Insurance.

PITI Ratio: Compares the amount of the monthly income to the amount the borrower will owe each month in principal, interest, real estate tax and insurance on a mortgage. Lenders use it in deciding whether to give the borrower a loan. Also called "debt to income" (DTI) ratio.

Planned Unit Development (PUD): A housing project that may consist of any combination of homes (one-family to four-family), condominiums, and various other styles. In a PUD, often the individual unit and the land upon which it sits are owned by the unit/homeowner; however, the homeowner's association owns common facilities.

Pre-Approval: A process in which a customer provides all of the appropriate information on income, debts and assets that will be used to make a credit only loan decision. The customer typically has not identified a property to be purchased, however, a specific sales price and loan amount are used to make a loan decision. (The sales price and loan amount are based on customer assumptions)

Pre-Qualification: A process designed to assist a customer in determining a maximum sales price, loan amount and PITI payment they are qualified for. A pre-qualification is not considered a loan approval. A customer would provide basic information (income, debts, assets) to be used to determine the maximum sales price, etc. Pre-qualifications are not nearly as valuable to you as a pre-approval.

Prepaid Expenses or Prepaids: The term used to describe the funds the Lender requires to be deposited to establish the escrow account for taxes and insurance at the time of closing (also refers to Prepaid Interest).

Prepaid Interest: Interest that the borrower pays the lender before it becomes due.

Prepayment: A loan repayment made in advance of its contractual due date.

Prepayment Penalty: A penalty under a Note, Mortgage or Deed of Trust imposed when the loan is paid before its maturity date.

Principal and Interest: Two components of a monthly mortgage payment. Principal refers to the portion of the monthly payment that reduces the remaining balance for the mortgage. Interest is the fee charged for borrowing money.

Principal Balance: The outstanding balance of a mortgage, not counting interest.

Principal, Interest, Real Estate Tax, Insurance Payment: The total mortgage payment which includes principal, interest, taxes and insurance.

Private Mortgage Insurance (PMI): Insurance against a loss by a lender in the event of default by a borrower (mortgagor). A private insurance company issues this insurance. The premium is paid by the borrower and is included in the mortgage payment.

Processing: Gathering the loan application and all required supporting documents (including the property appraisal, credit report, credit history, and income and expenses) so that a lender can consider the borrower for a loan.

Promissory Note: A document in which the borrower promises to pay a stated amount on a specific date. The note normally states the name of the lender, the terms of payment and any interest rate.

Property Taxes: Taxes assessed on real estate. Property taxes are based on valuations by local and or state governments.

Purchase Agreement: A written agreement between a buyer and seller of real property, that states the price and terms of the sale.

Purchase Price: The total amount paid for a home.

Qualifying Income Ratios: Income analysis used by lenders in deciding whether to offer the borrower a loan. One type of analysis compares only the amount of the proposed monthly mortgage payment to the monthly income. Another compares the amount of the total monthly payments (for example car, credit card and proposed mortgage payments) to the monthly income.

Rate Index: An index used to adjust the interest rate of an adjustable mortgage loan.

Real Estate Appreciation Rate: Percentage increase in the value of real estate, expressed at an annual rate.

Real Estate Settlement Procedures Act (RESPA): A consumer protection law that requires, among other things, lenders to give borrowers advance notice of closing costs.

Realtor: A person licensed to negotiate and transact the sale of real estate on behalf of the property owner. A real estate broker or associate must hold active membership in a real estate board affiliated with the National Association of Realtors.

Recording Fee: The amount paid to the recorder's office in order to make a document a matter of public record.

Regulation Z: Federal Reserve regulation issued under the Truth-in-Lending Act, which, among other things, requires that a credit purchaser be advised in writing of all costs connected with the credit portion of the loan.

Rental Payment: A payment made to use another's property. The amount of the rent is determined in a contract and is typically paid monthly.

Renters Insurance: Insurance against perils which are commonly covered in policies described as a "Renters Policy".

Repayment: The payment of a mortgage loan over a period of time established when the loan is originated.

Rescind: To avoid or cancel in such a way as to treat the contract or other object of the rescission as if it never existed.

Sales Contract: A written agreement between parties stating all terms and conditions of a sale.

Savings Rate: The interest rate a person expects to earn on a savings account or investment account.

Secondary Market: An informal market where existing mortgages are bought and sold. It is the traditional aftermarket for mortgage loans that brings together lenders that sell mortgages with lenders, investors and agencies that buy mortgages.

Seller Contribution: The seller may be paying some or all of the borrower's cost. The amount of the contribution has limitations.

Selling Costs: The costs incurred in selling a home. This could include Realtor expenses and other miscellaneous expenses such as painting or minor repairs to prepare the home for sale.

Servicing: All the management and operational procedures that the mortgage company handles for the life of the loan, up through foreclosure if necessary, including: collecting the mortgage payments, ensuring that the taxes and insurance charges are paid promptly, and sending an annual report on the mortgage and escrow accounts.

Servicing Released: A stipulation in the agreement for the sale of mortgages in which the Lender is not responsible for servicing the loan.

Servicing Retained: A loan sale in which the original lender's servicing department continues to service the loan after the sale to a secondary institution or investor.

Settlement Statement: Also referred to as a HUD-1 Settlement Statement. The complete breakdown of costs involved in the real estate transaction for both the seller and buyer.

Single-Family Attached Home: A single-family dwelling that is attached to other single-family dwellings.

Single-Family Detached Home: A freestanding dwelling for a single family

Survey: A measurement of land, prepared by a registered land surveyor, showing the location of the land with reference to known points, its dimensions and the location and dimensions of any improvements.

Subordinate Financing: An additional lien against the real estate securing borrower's first mortgage. This lien takes second priority to the first mortgage.

Subsequent Rate Adjustment – Maximum rate decrease: In association with an Adjustable Rate Mortgage loan, this is the most the interest rate can decrease when it is scheduled for reevaluation and possible adjustment.

Subsequent Rate Adjustment – Maximum rate increase: In association with an Adjustable Rate Mortgage loan, this is the most the interest rate can increase when it is scheduled for reevaluation and possible adjustment.

Subsequent Rate Adjustment – Next ARM Adjustment Date: In association with an Adjustable Rate Mortgage loan, this is the date scheduled for the next reevaluation and possible adjustment.

Subsequent Rate Adjustment – Rate Change Frequency: In association with an Adjustable Rate Mortgage loan, this is the frequency in which possible adjustments may be made to the interest rate amount for Adjustable Rate Mortgages after the initial adjustment.

Tax Rates: Tax Rates are typically thought of as those levied by the federal government and some states based on a person's income. Federal income tax rates vary depending on a person's adjusted gross income. In the real estate world, Tax Rate typically refers to your Property Tax Rate.

Tax Savings: The amount saved on taxes by itemizing deductions on income tax returns.

Title: The evidence to the right to or ownership in property. In the case of real estate, the documentary evidence of ownership is the title deed, which specifies in whom the legal state is vested and the history of ownership and transfers. Title may be acquired through purchase, inheritance, devise, gift or through the foreclosure of a mortgage.

Title Insurance Policy: A contract by which the insurer, usually a title company, indicates who has legal title and agrees to pay the insured a specific amount of any loss caused by clouds, claims or defects of title to real estate, which the insured has an interest as owner, mortgagee or otherwise.

(a) Owner's Title Policy: Usually issued to the landowner himself. The owner's title insurance policy is bought and paid for only once and then continues in force without any further payment. Owner's Title Insurance policies are not assignable.

(b) Mortgagee's Title Policy: Issued to the mortgagee and terminates when the mortgage debt is paid. In the event of foreclosure, or if the mortgagee acquires title from the mortgagor in lieu of foreclosure, the policy continues in force, giving continued protection against any defects of title which existed at, or prior to, the date of the policy.

Treasury Bills: Interest bearing U.S. Government obligations sold at a weekly sale. The change in interest rates paid on these obligations is frequently used as the Rate Index for Adjustable Mortgage Loans.

Truth in Lending (TIL): The name given to the federal statutes and regulations (Regulation Z) which are designed primarily to insure that prospective Borrowers of credit received credit and cost information before concluding a loan transaction.

Underwriting (Mortgage Loans): The process of evaluating a loan application to determine the risk involved for the lender. It involves an analysis of the borrower's creditworthiness and the quality of the property itself.

Verification of Deposit (VOD): Form used in mortgage lending to verify the deposits or assets of a prospective borrower when monthly statements are unavailable or unusable.

Verification of Employment (VOE): Form used in mortgage lending to verify the employment and income of a prospective borrower when pay stubs and W2 forms are unavailable or unusable.

Verification of Mortgage (VOM): Form used in mortgage lending to verify the existing mortgage balance, monthly payments and late payments, if any.

Verification of Rent: Form used in mortgage lending to verify monthly rents paid and late payments, if any.

Conclusion

Congratulations! You're substantially closer to being a home owner than you were before you started reading this book!

Thank you taking the time out of your busy schedule to read this book. I hope that the information and insider secrets that I have shared with you will help you and your family can reach your dream of home ownership.

You now have the knowledge and information you need to get started towards your goal of home ownership. But you have to take the next step. From this point forward, it is up to you to achieve your goal.

So get out there and grab your piece of the American Dream.

About the Author

Mark Kennedy first entered the financial services industry in 1991 and helped open his first mortgage company in 1993. In 2000 he became a partner in one of the nation's largest specialty mortgage companies. By 2005, he was being called upon to provide consulting services to banks and lenders nationwide that needed his expertise in marketing, customer service and process management.

Over the course of two decades, he has helped thousands of individuals and families buy or build their dream homes, often with little or no money down.

Additionally, his clients regularly came to him with credit issues or other problems that caused them to be previously denied loans. With his nearly 20 years as a mortgage and financing professional, he has learned credit secrets that only a few industry insiders know (and even fewer share).

Mark loves to expose the secrets and myths of the financing and credit world. And, although the credit bureaus and his competitors may not like it, his clients appreciate the honesty and candor with which he approaches his business.

The first edition of *How to Buy a House The Right Way* (first edition, 2006) was wildly popular among consumers seeking to buy their first home. Now, with its second printing (January, 2012), this book continues to provide the most current information available on home buying for first timers.

This book has been updated to account for all of the many changes in the mortgage and real estate market that have taken place since it was first published in 2006.

From The Smart Living Series:

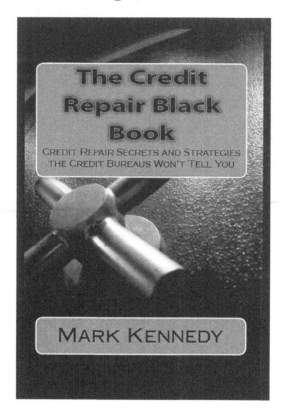

The Credit Repair Black Book
Credit Repair Secrets and Strategies the Credit Bureaus Won't Tell You

Available at Amazon in Paperback or Kindle Version.